The Secrets of Word-of-Mouth Marketing

The Secrets of Word-of-Mouth Marketing

How to Trigger Exponential Sales Through Runaway Word of Mouth

By
George Silverman
President and Founder
Market Navigation, Inc.

AMACOM

American Management Association

New York ■ Atlanta ■ Boston ■ Chicago ■ Kansas City ■ San Francisco ■ Washington, D.C.
Brussels ■ Mexico City ■ Tokyo ■ Toronto

Special discounts on bulk quantities of AMACOM books are available
to corporations, professional associations, and other organizations.
For details, contact Special Sales Department, AMACOM, an imprint
of AMA Publications, a division of American Management Association,
1601 Broadway, New York, NY 10019 Tel.: 212-903-8316
Fax: 212-903-8083

This publication is designed to provide accurate and authoritative information in regard to the subject matter covered. It is sold with the understanding that the publisher is not engaged in rendering legal, accounting, or other
professional service. If legal advice or other expert assistance is required, the
services of a competent professional person should be sought.

Library of Congress Cataloging-in-Publication Data

Silverman, George, 1942-
    The secrets of word-of mouth marketing : how to trigger expontential
    sales through runaway word of mouth / by George Silverman
        p. cm.
    Includes index.
    ISBN 0-8144-7072-6 (pbk.)
        1. Word-of-mouth advertising. 2. Marketing. I. Title.

    HF5827.95 .R67 2000
    658.8—dc21   00-067635

Printing number
10 9 8 7 6 5 4 3 2 1

Contents

v

The "Ultimate" Word-of-Mouth Program • How I
First Harnessed Word-of-Mouth

Acknowledgments

It took about thirty years and more than 6000 focus groups, word-of-mouth sessions and experts sessions, as well as the design of countless word-of-mouth marketing campaigns, to accumulate the knowledge that is distilled into the following pages. Not all of my clients will be happy that I am finally divulging (in a general way, without giving away any of *their* secrets) the secrets that have made their products so successful, in many cases causing record-breaking sales gains.

I believe that this book is the beginning of a historic turning point in marketing, which will spawn an entire industry, the word-of-mouth marketing industry.

I'd like to acknowledge the people who contributed to the development of this book, both out of this sense of history, and especially out of a sense of gratitude.

My father, Irving Silverman, in a sense taught me everything I ever learned about marketing (see *"[Almost] Everything I Know About Marketing, I Learned In My Father's Drug Store,"* in Chapter 10 in this book), particularly the idea of building a business by "cultivating the customer" to stimulate word of mouth.

I was fortunate to have had a series of mentors in my life, each of whom allowed me to study their greatness firsthand, and maybe even have a little rub off. Ayn Rand, in my opinion the greatest novelist (*Atlas Shrugged, The Fountainhead*), philosopher, and thinker to have ever lived, in a series of provocative conversations lasting several years, taught me (among many other things) how to think both analytically and creatively at the same time and how to stay clear even when I was confused. Her private course in non-fiction writing, for a small number of people who were lucky enough to attend, was a masterpiece that I am hoping will be published soon. Hiam Ginnott (author of *Between Parent and Child*), one of the greatest child psychologists of our time, taught me (I hope) how to communicate forcefully but respectfully, and how to be a gracious expert. Tony Slydini, my magic mentor, widely regarded by knowledgeable magicians as the greatest close-up magician of the twentieth century, inspired me to go beyond the limits of our ordinary assumptions, to use playfulness, wonder, amazement, and astonishment constructively, and to seek to attain a breakthrough level in everything, no matter how simple or ambitious. A part of you all live on inside of me.

My partners (in many senses of that word) also contributed immeasurably. Of course, my ultimate partner, my wife, Dr. Marla Silverman, is a constant source of love and encouragement, while being an uncompromisingly accurate and constructive sounding board and mirror. I also thank my children, Ilyssa and Eric. The three of you make it all worthwhile. I thank you particularly for putting up with my detachment and grumpiness during the writing process.

Eve Zukergood, my partner in Market Navigation, has been with me during almost the entire journey of developing the Word of Mouth Navigation System. She has ceaselessly encouraged the vision of the possibilities, as well as helped me develop, refine, and clarify most of its ideas. She kept our company together operationally and expanded the business while both she and I experimented with new approaches and ideas.

Ron Richards, President of ResultsLab in San Francisco, a former partner, turned me on to thinking about word of mouth explicitly. He had the vision to see that word of mouth is the driving force of marketing, and he has continually offered constructive suggestions and breakthrough new ideas.

Several advisors have also made extremely important contributions. Most of them are part of our informal consulting group of independent consultants who recommend each other and sometimes work on projects together: Robert Keiper, who consults on clear communication in both writing and presenting, has rewritten some of my writings, and in so doing has taught me how to write more clearly and concisely. The challenges of his independent mind have forced me to clarify and simplify, over many decades, what I mistakenly thought was clear. The late Bernadette Tracy, an expert on Internet trends, has also been a continual source of inspiration, encouragement, rethinking, and clarity. She was the one who would get me back to Earth when I was lost in the stratosphere. Bill Cope, a creative idea generation consultant, has taken the mystery out of creativity, but not the wonder. Brad Boyer, president of Bradley Dean Associates, has continued to work with me on the clarity of my presentations. Mike Basch, former vice president of Service for Federal Express, has been an inspiration and a joy to bounce ideas off of. Marianna Maddocks, one of my first clients about thirty years ago and close friend, expert in human resources, and so much more, is a constant source of positive energy, good will, and an occasional, well-deserved kick in the butt. Kimberly Nicholson, President of Marketing Resource, is also a continuing source of professional collaboration, encouragement, good cheer, and collegial support. So are Pam Colgate, who never fails to lift my spirits, even when I'm on a high, and Gary Kash, Grandmaster of Product Positioning, a brilliant source of insight, intelligence, and creativity.

A lot changed when I read *Million Dollar Consulting*, by Alan Weiss. His principles work. I know. I liked his books so much, I hired him as a consultant. It was he who got me to finish the book and see how to tie consulting payments to value, not work or time expended. I heartily recommend anything he is involved with.

Jay Abraham, entrepreneurial marketing guru, has also been an inspiration, an example, and an important source of validation. Aaron Altman has read and reread several incarnations of this book, and his contributions have also contributed to many of the insights. Gay Botway, who helped me start Market Navigation, was also a constant source of encouragement.

Anne Scordo single-handedly coordinated many of our experts and other word-of-mouth conferences, as well as continually finding spelling and grammatical errors that, I could swear, weren't there when I gave her the material.

Wendy Keller, President of ForthWright Literary Agency and Speakers Bureau, my literary agent, has been a continual source of inspiration, encouragement, optimism, and reassurance. It's very difficult to write and sell a book. It is an abstract enterprise that is fraught with crises of confidence. She seems to know just what to say to keep me in great spirits and raise my sights, while being brutally honest about what to expect. She is responsive, straightforward, and effective. She saw the potential of the book long before others. I hope that she is right. I hope that she is also right about my next book on "Customer Decision Acceleration." If you're looking for an agent, look no further.

Which brings me to the folks at AMACOM. Ellen Kadin, my editor, has been most perceptive in selecting this book and has been very encouraging about its prospects. I hope that she too is right. She, Wendy, and Ellen's colleagues must be very perceptive indeed: they like my magic effects.

There are many people who will influence and contribute to the Word of Mouth Navigation System in the future, including—hopefully—you the reader. To you all, I thank you in advance.

The Secrets of Word-of-Mouth Marketing

The Calf-Path

One day through the primeval wood
A calf walked home, as good calves should;
But made a trail all bent askew,
A crooked trail as all calves do.

Since then three hundred years have fled,
And I infer the calf is dead.
But still he left behind his trail,
And thereby hangs my moral tale:

The trail was taken up next day
By a lone dog that passed that way;
And then a wise bellwether sheep
Pursued the trail o'er hill and glade
Through those old woods a path was made.

And many men wound in and out
And dodged and turned and bent about
And uttered words of righteous wrath
Because 'twas such a crooked path;
But still they followed—do not laugh —
The first migrations of that calf,
And through this winding wood-way stalked
Because he wobbled when he walked.

This forest path became a lane
That bent and turned and turned again;
This crooked lane became a road,
Where many a horse with his load
Toiled on beneath the burning sun,
And traveled some three miles in one.
And thus a century and a half
They trod the footsteps of that calf.

The years passed on in swiftness fleet,
The road became a village street;
And thus, before men were aware,
A city's crowded thoroughfare.
And soon the central street was this
Of a renowned metropolis;
And men two centuries and a half
Trod in the footsteps of that calf.

Each day a hundred thousand rout
Followed this zigzag calf about
And o'er his crooked journey went
The traffic of a continent.

A hundred thousand men were led
By one calf near three centuries dead.
They followed still his crooked way,
And lost one hundred years a day;
For thus such reverence is lent
To well-established precedent.

For men are prone to go it blind,
Along the calf-paths of the mind;
And work away from sun to sun,
To do what other men have done.

They follow in the beaten track,
And out and in, and forth and back,
And still their devious course pursue,
To keep the path that others do.

They keep the path a sacred groove,
Along which all their lives they move.
But how the wise old wood gods laugh,
Who saw that first primeval calf!
—by SAM WALTER FOSS, 1895

Please feel free to copy this poem and give it to a friend or colleague. It's an example of one of the secrets of word-of-mouth marketing: Give people something valuable, something that's an example of your product or service, or your quality, or your good taste, with your name on it, and that they are likely to pass on. You can also get a copy of the poem electronically at our Web site: www.mnav.com/calf-path.htm. As an experiment, it will be interesting to see how much this obscure poem gets passed around. Another secret of word-of-mouth marketing is to appeal to the desire to have fun, in this case by participating in a beneficial experiment in which people will bring in other people.

You should include the following reference in any fax or photocopy of the poem you provide to someone:

> Quoted in *The Secrets of Word-of-Mouth Marketing: How to Trigger Exponential Sales through Runaway Word of Mouth*, George Silverman, AMACOM, New York, 2001. This book will keep you off the crooked road of conventional marketing and set you on the "straight and narrow path" to greatly increased sales with less marketing expenditure.

Introduction

The Copernican Revolution in Marketing

If you simply observe the sky, it is obvious—but untrue—that the Sun revolves around the Earth. It is just as obvious—but just as untrue—that marketing revolves around advertising, selling, and promotion.

Both are illusions: things that appear compellingly true but aren't. I have been a serious student of illusion since childhood, in the hope that becoming an expert in the principles of illusion (I prefer to be called a close-up illusionist rather than a magician) will make me see reality more clearly. In that spirit I can confidently report to you that most of marketing is illusion. In two ways.

First, much of modern-day marketing is about *creating illusions about products*, variously called product image, positioning, brand identity, and other buzzwords. There is nothing wrong with that, since much of life is about creating legitimate illusion. For instance, all art is illusion. A painting is only some smears of paint. But what smears! They are capable of evoking images of people and inspiring intense emotion. Film is just a series of stills (themselves illusions, being only arrangements of colored film emulsion or videotape electronic impulses) run at a fast speed to create the illusion of motion. Actors are creating the illusion that they are someone else. Magicians are actors playing the part of people who can do the impossible.

So, there is nothing really wrong with creating vivid images about products that make people feel good about using them. There is nothing wrong with painting a vivid picture of what it will be like to receive the benefits of a product.

But much of marketing is illusion in a second, more dangerous sense. Much of marketing is itself an illusion: It isn't really what it seems to be. Marketers are spending huge amounts of money for the Emperor's New Clothes. Let me explain.

The illusion is that your marketing elements are *selling* your product. The reality is that people are *buying*, often not necessarily in response to you, but in response to what they hear from other independent sources. The illusion is that they are buying in response to what you are saying. There is a large body of research that shows that people gather information from your marketing materials, including salespeople and advertising, then talk it over with their friends. They buy in response to what other people say about the product.

Most marketers have only recently realized that *getting the customer* to sell their products is the best way to increase sales. In other words, the world of marketing really revolves around word of mouth, not around sales and advertising. Word of mouth is not just a welcome by-product of good marketing. You talk, people listen. *Then they talk it over* with their friends, family, and trusted advisors. Then they buy, but not before talking about your product. While they are trying your product, they talk. After they have committed to your product, they talk some more.

Getting people to talk often, favorably, to the right people in the right way about your product is far and away the most important thing that you can do as a marketer.

This, then, is the essence of word-of-mouth marketing. Word of mouth is the center of the marketing universe and certainly the method of choice for selling products.

There's an old saying that, "If all you have is a hammer, everything begins to look like a nail." Everything in marketing tends to be looked at from the point of view of traditional marketing, because marketers believe that this is all they have. Let's look at an example.

A CASE IN POINT

In my speeches and workshops, I almost always show the audience a pair of dice. I ask someone in the front row to call out the sum of the two dice as I roll them a few times. The numbers will be something like this: 7, 9, 3, 9, 11, 5, 3, 11, 7, 9, 5. When I ask people what is unusual about the numbers that are being thrown, someone eventually shouts out that they are all odd numbers. I explain that there are four ways that such ordinary-looking dice could always total odd numbers: (1) magnets, (2) shaved dice, (3) weighted dice, or (4) one die is all odd numbers, the other die is all even numbers. In fact, all four methods are used by dice cheats. For my demonstration, I use method #4. My point is, how could you tell that I'm using even and odd dice, when they look perfectly OK? You can only see three sides of a cube at a time, and the way the dice are set up, there is a different number visible on each side. The only way you can tell is to pick them up, or *change your perspective*, to see that on one die there is a 2 opposite a 2, a 4 opposite a 4, and a 6 opposite a 6, and on the other die a 1 opposite a 1, a 3 opposite a 3 and a 5 opposite a 5. The point that this demonstration illustrates is that *the only way you can get a true picture in any situation is to look from many perspectives, to change your viewpoint, to consider things from different angles.*

Word of mouth is just one perspective, or viewpoint, from which to view marketing. There are also traditional ways of looking at it, such as advertising, sales, or promotion. No particular *viewpoint* is more valid than the other. Orientations, viewpoints, perspectives, angles, standpoints, and points of view are just places from which to look at things. There is nothing inherently right or wrong about looking at things from a particular perspective. There is, however, something profoundly wrong with looking at things from only one viewpoint. You will get an incomplete picture. On the other hand, the ideas, conclusions, and beliefs that come from looking at things from another angle may be right or wrong, but the place from which you look is just that, only a place.

Orientations do, however, differ greatly in how *fruitful* they are in helping us know and organize the world. Some are highly illuminating, such as "How would this look to a child, or to someone who didn't understand the field?" or "How does this look from my customer's point of view?" Singularly *unfruitful* lines of approach, or viewpoints, are "How can I sell my product?" or "How can I get people to use my product?" These last two are the usual approaches to marketing. They aren't wrong, but if they are our *only* perspectives, they tend to lead us to neglect the customer's viewpoint, and therefore lead us into ineffective ways of marketing. They are an invitation to put on blinders.

The only way to know something with any depth and create anything worthwhile is to look at it from more than one perspective. Walk around it, look from above and below, get inside it, imagine it differently, or reinvent it. Now what does this have to do with word of mouth?

Everything.

Keep whatever orientations and perspectives—even illusions—that have worked for you in the past, such as the advertising and/or sales perspectives. But in addition, look at all of your marketing as a *word-of-mouth generating system.* If, as is true for most products, it's the word of mouth that triggers the sales, isn't it important to look at what triggers the word of mouth?

What if all elements of marketing, such as sales, advertising, and direct mail, were not oriented toward *directly persuading* people to use the product? Instead, what if your marketing elements were organized around *causing people to talk about the product* in a way that would get them to use more, and get their friends and colleagues to use more?

Sometimes the "long way 'round" can be the fastest. In fact, going after word of mouth directly is not the long way around. It's what happens anyway: Marketing leads to word of mouth, which leads to sales. Why not try organizing everything around word of mouth, since it's the central part of the mix?

There are many ways to accomplish this, such as through testimonial ads, case studies of how customers used the product successfully, endorsements, and the like. These are usually very effective methods, which is why they are used and often overused.

Word-of-Mouth Generation System

What I'm urging you to consider is a total approach. What if *all parts* of your marketing were focused single-mindedly on one goal: getting people to talk favorably—in the right way—about your product(s)? When you look at your marketing system from this perspective—*as a word-of-mouth generation system*—you will see it in a whole different light, which reveals many opportunities. It's like going backstage and seeing how the illusion really works.

For instance, if you look at your marketing communications, you will almost always see elements that couldn't possibly generate word of mouth, or elements that just couldn't survive from one person to another. For instance, you may see communications that flatly assert unsubstantiated "facts," in a brute force attempt to convince skeptics, instead of employing, say, simple quotes from experts and/or users. Or you may see blunders, such as materials with "photocopier unfriendly" dark-colored backgrounds, which would make it impossible to copy the material and give it to a friend. Does your company have an ironclad rule that all brochures have to survive multiple recopying, so that customers can send materials to friends? If not, you aren't word-of-mouth oriented, even if you keep telling everyone that your product depends on word of mouth.

I may not be able to quantify how many opportunities are lost or how much more effective most marketing mixes could be made if they were viewed from the perspective of word of mouth, but I can say that it is routine to be able to increase sales tenfold (yes, ten times, exponentially) by organizing marketing around the goal of—first and foremost—generating word of mouth.

Word of Mouth Is More Important Now Than Ever Before

It is the Information Age, and we are inundated with overwhelming quantities of information. We don't have time to investigate and deliberate.

That's why traditional advertising is on the decline. TV networks are losing viewers. Magazines are in trouble. Broadcast and print ads are costing more and producing poorer results. Traditional sales people are almost dinosaurs. People just don't have the time for sorting through the information overload.

Therefore, word of mouth becomes a necessary time saver. It's much easier to let other people cut through the information, distill and refine it, filter it, and then give us the benefit of their experience.

The good news is that the Information Age contains the seeds of its own solutions: The very media that threaten to overwhelm us are themselves the means for coping with the problems they create. Virtually any information channel is itself also potentially a word-of-mouth channel. So, as the information increases, so does the access to the word of mouth that will cut through the information overload.

As a result, we will become increasingly dependent upon word of mouth to cut through the clutter, to tell us what is most important, what to pay attention to, to bring us the benefit of experience and to bring us filtered information, particularly from experts. E-mail, electronic group collaboration, chat rooms, forums, Web sites, and teleconferences, while threatening to overwhelm us, will bring us the word of mouth that will actually save us time and make us money.

CHAPTER 1

Dominating Your Market by Shortening the Customer Decision Cycle

Let's start from the beginning. What are we trying to do as marketers?

Put simply, we are trying—through a variety of means—to get lots of people to buy our products—repeatedly, in large quantities and at rewarding prices. We are trying to bring our products to people in the most profitable manner possible, both for our customers and ourselves.

How do we accomplish this? It's widely believed that there are only three ways to increase sales: increase the number of customers, increase the dollar amount each customer spends per purchase (higher prices and/or larger orders), or increase the frequency with which the customer buys. Ask virtually any marketing expert, consult the marketing books, and they will all tell you that this exhausts the possibilities.

But the *most important* way of increasing sales and dominating a market has never, to my knowledge, ever been written about: *Increase the speed with which decisions are made.* You heard it here first. Let's take a look at this concept in detail, because decision acceleration is the most powerful way to dominate a market, and word of mouth is the most powerful way to accelerate decisions.

Amazingly, marketing success is determined more by the time it takes your customers to decide on your product than by any other single factor. Decision speed is more powerful than positioning, image, value, customer satisfaction, guarantees, or even product superiority, because focusing on it forces you to organize these factors, and many more, into the most potent combination possible.

Why Decision Speed Determines Product Success

Decision speed is the time it takes your customers to go from initial awareness to enthusiastic full use and recommendation of your product or service. This in turn is governed by the simplicity, ease, and sometimes the fun of the decision process.

Obviously, the company that makes its products easier to decide on will acquire customers faster and increase market share faster. But increased decision speed causes much larger changes in market share than might be obvious. In fact, it's the key to dominating your market.

Accelerated decisions are in a different class from other marketing program adjustments. While most marketing changes—at best—provide incremental market share increases (typically 10 to 30 percent), faster decision cycles can improve market share by *orders of magnitude (10 to 100 times).*

Why Speed Equals Multiplied Sales

Suppose there are five similar products competing in a new category. All things being equal, they will each eventually capture a 20 percent market share. Say the decision cycle time for these products is about one year.

Now suppose that you are competitor #1, and you find a way to make several of the time-consuming steps in that decision cycle easier for your prospects, cutting the decision time in half. What happens to your and the other competitors' market share?

> *Amazingly, marketing success is determined more by the time it takes your customers to decide on your product than by any other single factor. Decision speed is more powerful than positioning, image, value, customer satisfaction, guarantees, or even product superiority, because focusing on it forces you to organize these factors, and many more, into the most potent combination possible.*

Obviously, if your product achieves its expected one-year market share in six months, it will have effectively doubled the market window of opportunity, giving you the time and resources to capture another 20 percent market share in the remaining six months. This would give your product a 40 percent share at year's end, with the four other competitors sharing the remainder, at 15 percent each.

But even that triumph is not the whole story. It leaves out the powerful effect of word of mouth and assumes each prospect makes a solitary decision. When you increase the decision speed for your prospects by 100 percent, you not only get customers sooner, you turn those customers into zealous advocates for your product before the competitors have a similar opportunity. Why would your user endorsements be any better than those from competitors? First because they are available sooner, but second, and more important, your endorsements will be supported by the targeted, persuasive information you selected and provided to shorten the decision cycle in the first place!

With this kind of decision support, the first marketing months can generate such evangelism among early adopters that a 40 percent market share could be too conservative a goal. A more likely outcome could be a 60 percent to 80 percent market share for your product, a 10 percent share for product #2, with the others splitting the remainder. This isn't pie in the sky. Most marketers will recognize that this is the pattern for many products.

How Decision Time Can Be Cut in Half

Can you really cut the decision time in half? Isn't that unrealistic? Yes. My experience has shown that this is *too conservative*. Usually, you can cut decision time by way more than half when you precisely map the customers' decision processes, reduce *decision friction*, and remove the bottlenecks by concentrating on the communications that will really move people to action.

Here follow some examples, but keep in mind that people who have used decision acceleration and word-of-mouth campaigns are understandably secretive about them. Word of mouth—especially intentionally caused word of mouth—is an amazingly powerful secret weapon that people want to keep secret. In fact, the very fact that people might think that certain information delivered by word of mouth was "planted" would destroy its credibility. So, I have to disguise many of the examples in this book. Some examples are simply unidentified, others are changed in detail but not in principle, and others still are amalgams of several different programs.

A CASE IN POINT

People were holding back from using a major new drug because they were worried about the dangers of its use. It turned out that these dangers were well founded. The product had actually killed nine people. We got users of the product as well as experts, who had been using the premarket version and the marketed version, to talk about its safety, but also its potential danger if not used properly. People stopped waiting for the other person to use it and jumped to get its benefits immediately. It turned out that it was easy to use safely with certain precautions, and sales skyrocketed (more than 700 percent).

A CASE IN POINT

In another case, an industrial machine's prices were more than 30 percent higher than the competition, but the overall costs were much lower because it had fewer and cheaper repairs, was supported by expensive training, and the company did not oversell more or fancier equipment than the customer needed. But people could not justify it to their bosses. Some did not know how to even begin to justify it. Others were waiting until they could get around to "doing a study." This wait turned out to be years in duration. The company turned years into weeks by getting some of its most enthusiastic customers to make their studies public and serve as references. They even prepared a slide show template and sample spreadsheets that their prospects could modify to present to their bosses.

Choosing a product is not a single decision; it's a series of decisions, often an *extended* series. Some choices along the way can be fast and easy to make, but many require time, attention, and effort in gathering and verifying information, weighing options, testing and evaluating results, and persuading others. I call this time, attention, and effort "decision friction." The process of deciding is slowed by each of these time-consuming bottlenecks and friction points.

If you can *identify and minimize just a few of those decision bottlenecks* for your customers, you can reduce their decision time by more than half, thereby *multiplying* the sales and market share of your product or service. In my thirty-plus years as a marketing consultant, I've seen it happen for products and services of every description, whether the decision cycle for the product was measured in years, months, weeks, days, or minutes.

A CASE IN POINT

A complicated piece of machinery required extensive research to buy, usually taking about six months. It then needed to be compared to the alternatives, which also took months. Then it had to be tried, which took about a year. Then it had to be rolled out gradually, with training. Another year. The whole thing was compressed into about eight weeks by holding a seminar/training program, then following it up by audio teleconferences. The decision makers were given the material that would have taken them months to find, shown how to evaluate it, given extensive (and flattering) competitive materials, and encouraged to try one against the other—all in a carefully structured trial that kept several prospects in touch with each other and with customers, with a hotline to third-party experts. This word of mouth, applied to several critical bottlenecks in the decision process, cut the decision time by multiples, while at the same time showing that the company had nothing to hide.

The Secret to Shortening the Customer's Decision Cycle

Shorten the decision cycle by making the decisions easier for the prospect, by focusing on their particular decision roadblocks, bottlenecks, friction points, and rough spots. It's this ridiculously simple marketing idea that's at the root of my entire approach to marketing. It's one of those ideas that is simple, obvious, compelling, and almost totally ignored, both in theory and practice. Decision acceleration is not written about by marketing gurus, and it is not thought about by product managers formulating product strategy. It will turn into your secret weapon. This is probably the most important paragraph in this book and I hope to publish a book on it as well.

Decision Acceleration System

To make the decision *easier*, think of your sales people, product materials, presentations, seminars, press releases, hot lines—in fact, every aspect of your marketing program—not as sales communications, but as a *Decision Acceleration System* for your customers and prospects.

To turn your marketing into a Decision Acceleration System, make the product:

- Benefits, claims, and promises obvious and compelling

- Information clear, balanced, and credible

- Comparisons reveal meaningful differences

- Trial easy

- Evaluations crystal clear and simple

- Guarantees ironclad and generous

- Testimonials and other word-of-mouth marketing relevant and believable

- Delivery, training, and support superior

When customers have information that makes a decision *easy*, they make it *quickly*. When a company makes it easy for me to decide on their product, not only do I buy the product, I also feel gratitude and a sense of loyalty to the company that gave me the easy choice. Full, balanced information about a product or service—including clear product comparisons, guarantees, and a commitment to support, all provided in the right sequence—enhances the value of the product and gives it a competitive advantage. Stated another way, the product with the better decision-support system often has the competitive edge, even if the product itself is not superior.

I am the world's worst salesman, therefore, I must make it easy for people to buy.   —F. W. Woolworth

This isn't just theory. It is a fact of life for every product or service, whether it's a simple consumer packaged goods product or the most complex medical, industrial, financial, or agricultural device or service. If you make the decision easier, more prospects can select your product more quickly and with greater confidence, and overwhelming market dominance is often the result. Not just market share increases of 10 percent, 25 percent, or even 50 percent, but 10, 25, or 50 *times* the expected market share. For the very few who have discovered it, it's the best-kept secret weapon in marketing.

Sometimes a product comes along that is so obviously superior that it seems to "sell itself." (Even then you could say that it sold itself because the decision was so easy.) But most buying decisions take time and effort. If the information provided by the seller is inadequate, we must go searching on our own to make up the deficits. At best, the days, weeks, or months lost by those delays cause confusion (a form of decision friction) and thereby slow the product's growth, making it share the market with all the competitors. Your advantages get lost in the shuffle. These decision points accumulate, causing prospects to drop out of the decision cycle, and spell disaster for the product's success.

The Decision Is Much Too Important to Leave to the Customer

You need to structure the decision process for customers, and guide them through the twists and turns. Without active guidance, they will falter and flounder, and drown in a sea of information.

THE MOST IMPORTANT PASSAGE IN THIS BOOK

Shorten the decision cycle by making the decisions easier for the prospect, by focusing on their particular decision roadblocks, bottlenecks, friction points, and rough spots. It's this ridiculously simple marketing idea that's at the root of my entire approach to marketing. It's one of those ideas that is simple, obvious, compelling, and almost totally ignored, both in theory and practice. Decision acceleration is not written about by marketing gurus, and it is not thought about by product managers formulating product strategy. It will turn into your secret weapon.

The marketer can make the decision road a superhighway or a neglected, pothole-strewn byway. If the road smooths the way for prospects, the speed limit goes up and there can be enormous market-share gains. This makes decision acceleration the most critical element on the road to market success.

How Do You Do This?

Go to some of the better Web sites, like some of the Microsoft small business sites. These Web sites are not only giving information, they are *guiding people through the decision*. This means that they have different tracks for beginners and sophisticated people, they use comparison charts and rating sheets, and they make the information easy to understand and to lay out for comparisons.

They are models of simplicity and relevance. They have case studies and genuinely useful information from customers. They have discussion groups, toll-free numbers to get questions answered, ways to download trial software, application examples and help, and examples from industries like yours. Yet, they appear simple to the customer. Most other sites overwhelm you with a tidal wave of information, presented from their point of view, not from the struggling customers' perspectives. There are no signposts, no organizational help, no simplicity.

Why Is Decision Acceleration So Important?
Decision acceleration is the most important breakthrough in marketing. For the purpose of this book, it is important that you understand at least the basic concept of decision acceleration, because *what overwhelmingly has the greatest effect on accelerating customer decisions is word of mouth.*

CHAPTER 2

The Power of Word of Mouth

As we saw in the previous chapter, word of mouth is the most powerful way to make the decision easier and accelerate your prospects' decision process.

Understanding Word of Mouth

You have probably anticipated where this is going. Far and away the best way to make the decision easier is for a *trusted advisor to encourage the customer to use the product, i.e., word of mouth.* In ways that we will examine shortly, word of mouth cuts through the marketplace clutter—for buyer and seller alike—and makes it easier to make a decision.

Why easier? The best way to avoid work and still get something done is to have someone else do it. That's what advisors, experts, and peers do. It's a way of getting other people to put in the work and risk of gathering information and trying products. That way, you don't have to take the time, spend the resources, and incur the risks of doing it yourself.

Therefore:

■ The best way to *increase profits* is to *accelerate favorable product decisions.*

- The best way to *accelerate product decisions* is to *make them easier.*

- The best way to *make the decisions easier* is to *deliver word of mouth*, instead of confusing, low-credibility information in the form of advertising, salespeople, or other traditional marketing.

Every marketer realizes that word of mouth is the most powerful force in the marketplace. Almost no one realizes just how powerful *it really* is: Word of mouth is THOUSANDS of times as powerful as conventional marketing.

Now that may sound like a wild statement, but let's think about it. The average person is exposed to about 200 to 1000 sales communications a day. Every day, we are exposed to television commercials; print ads; drive time radio; billboards on buses, subways, roads, and buildings; telemarketers; direct mail pieces; salespeople; Internet banners; brochures; matchbook covers; airplane streamers; and blimps. If we read only a couple of magazines or newspapers, we may be exposed to hundreds of ads.

Word of mouth is thousands of times more powerful than conventional marketing.

Just how many of these ads do you respond to? Most people respond to a commercial communication once every few days, if that. That's once in several thousand exposures. And the response is rarely to purchase. It's usually to just get more information.

Now imagine that a friend calls you up to recommend a movie, book, or other product. You are likely to take his recommendation. You may not take every recommendation, but you'll probably take, on average, from one out of two to one out of five.

In other words, you are thousands of times more likely to act on a recommendation of a friend, colleague, or trusted advisor than you are to a commercial communication. And this action is often full purchase, not just getting more information! QED.

Think about it.

Word of Mouth: The Most Powerful Force in the Marketplace

Isn't it amazing how marketers are overlooking the obvious? Word of mouth is far and away the dominant force in the marketplace. Yet it is also the most neglected.

Companies have vice presidents of sales, advertising, and marketing. But if word of mouth is a more dominant force than any of these, why not make it the dominant marketing function? Yet, *there isn't a single vice president of word of mouth in any corporation in the country.* Why?

Presumably this is so because most people think that they can't do much about word of mouth. Most marketers believe, implicitly or explicitly, that word of mouth is out of their control. They believe that advertising and other marketing media can influence it, to be sure, but not directly.

The revelation that awaits them is that word of mouth can be in their control. Under the right circumstances, its unmatched power can be harnessed with a resulting stampede of customers to your products that cannot be stopped by your competitors.

Even those deaf to the bragging cries of the marketplace will listen to a friend.   —Paddi Lund

That's what this book is about.

Chances are, your product is influenced more by word of mouth than by anything else. You and your competitors put huge amounts of information into the marketplace in the form of marketing materials, promotions, and salespeople. All the while, your customers and prospects are engaging in word of mouth: They are talking over that information and helping each other decide what to do.

Word of mouth is much more credible than your most sincere salesperson. It is able to reach more people, and faster, than advertising and direct mail because it can spread like wildfire. It breaks through the clutter better than anything. As one highly successful marketer, Paddi Lund (probably the world's most successful dentist), put it: "Even those deaf to the bragging cries of the marketplace will listen to a friend."

Even more important than its credibility, reach, speed, and ability to break through the clutter, is its power to get people to *act*. In study after study, with almost every category of buyer, word of mouth has been shown to be what is known as the "proximal cause" of purchase—the most recent thing that happened just before purchase. In other words, the purchase trigger. What happens just prior to buying is very often a pressure-free conversation with a colleague or friend where the product is spoken of glowingly.

Most marketers recognize that people tend to make major purchases on the advice of trusted peers, advisors, or experts. In addition, word of mouth happens spontaneously, without you having to be there, and, unlike what is true of your other media, it doesn't cost you a dime.

If only you could harness it.

The Most Costly Oversight in Marketing

The idea that word of mouth can't be harnessed is probably the most dangerous and costly marketing oversight. It will surprise most marketers to find out that word of mouth can be produced and controlled at least as much as advertising, salespeople, PR, coupons, samples, promotions, and the other marketing media and tactics. However, like most other things in life, it can't be *completely* controlled.

It *can* be strongly influenced and even harnessed, and in that sense, controlled. I prefer to speak of harnessing word of mouth, since that implies very strong influence, short of total control. But how do we harness word of mouth?

Before we can harness it, we have to know the nature of the beast before there is any chance of taming it, harnessing it, and directing its power. There is a lot more to this strange and powerful force than is generally understood. We have to find a way to monitor and track it, to sneak up on it, and observe it. Then, and only then, can we learn to speed it up, change its direction, and turn it into a stampede toward our product.

Stalking the Beast: What Is This Strange Creature?

Word of mouth is one of those things that everybody thinks they understand, yet they soon realize that they are each talking about a different part of the elephant. Here's the bottom line:

> Word of mouth is communication about products and services between people who are perceived to be independent of the company providing the product or service, in a medium perceived to be independent of the company.

These communications can be conversations, or just one-way testimonials. They can be live or canned. They can be in person, by telephone, e-mail, listgroup, or any other means of communication. They can be one-to-one, one-to-many (broadcast), or group discussions. But the essential element is that they are from or among people who are perceived to have little commercial vested interest in persuading someone else to use the product and therefore no particular incentive to distort the truth in favor of the product or service.

In contrast, *advertising* is the communication of a message that is chosen, designed, and worded by the seller of the product or service, in a medium that is owned or rented. A *sales message* is a "company line" delivered by a representative of the company. On the other hand, word of mouth is originated by a third party and transmitted spontaneously in a way that is independent of the producer or seller. In word of mouth, both the message and the medium are independent. In that sense, PR is actually one form (by no means the only form) of word of mouth, since even though the original impetus of the message is not independent, the message is *perceived* as written by an independent party in an independent medium.

The Power of Word of Mouth: Independent Credibility

It is this *independence* that gives it much, but by no means all, of its power. If you ask most people why word of mouth is so powerful, they will tell you that it's because of its objective, independent, and "no ax to grind" and "no vested interest" nature. Why is that so important? Because a decision maker is more likely to get the *whole, undistorted truth* from an independent third party than from someone who has a vested interest in promoting the company point of view. It is this unique *credibility* that gives word of mouth much of its power.

That explains part of why word of mouth is often negative. When people ask someone about a product, they are likely to ask, "Had any trouble with X?" They know that it is only from an independent source that they are likely to get a straight answer, especially about negatives. In fact, it's the only place where the decision maker is likely to hear about the negatives of the product.

Another reason that word of mouth is often negative is that people are three to ten times more likely to tell others about a negative experience than a positive one. Many studies have shown that a satisfied customer is likely to tell approximately three people, whereas a dissatisfied customer is likely to tell approximately eleven people. This is often because the positive experiences are expected and soon forgotten, but the unresolved negatives get people angry and frustrated, energizing word of mouth. Studies have also shown that unexpected extraordinary service also causes strong positive word of mouth. In fact, some of the strongest and most frequent word of mouth is caused when dissatisfied customers are turned around by an extraordinary response to their expression of dissatisfaction.

So, as we have seen, word of mouth can be a powerful positive force because of its credibility, but it can also be destructive because of its negativity.

The Hidden Advantage of Word of Mouth: Experience Delivery

Experience Delivery is a second reason why word of mouth is so powerful, and it is even more important and useful than word of mouth's independent credibility. It is crucial to understand it, because it is the key to most of the power of word of mouth, and the key to channeling word of mouth in the right direction. It is truly a secret of word-of-mouth marketing, since—to my knowledge—no one has ever identified this as the central reason for word of mouth's power.

When a person is deliberating about purchasing a product, she reaches a point where she wants to try the product. Ideally, she wants to get low-risk, real-world experience using the product. Up until then, everything is informational, abstract, and somewhat removed from the real world. She has to know how the product will "actually work out in the real world." In other words, she needs *experience*.

What gives word of mouth most of its power is the fact that it is an experience-delivery mechanism.

There are only two ways to get experience: *directly or indirectly.* Now you would think that *direct experience*—actually trying the product—is the best teacher. But it is often the most costly in time, money, and risk of failure. Also, most people don't have the resources to try new products fully, in large numbers of situations, which keeps their experience base or sample small.

Indirect Experience

Indirect experience—that is, hearing about other people's experience—is actually much better than direct experience in many ways: Someone else is footing the bill and spending the time, and you can pool the experience of several people so as to have a greater sample. If the trial fizzles, their reputations are damaged, not yours. All in all, indirect, vicarious experience is a safer, better deal. Of course, it's not that black and white. Where it's feasible, you might "test-drive" the product a little yourself, and also talk with others about their experiences with it.

This sharing of risk—talking with others about the product, comparing experiences, and helping each other sort it all out—is the most powerful form of this most powerful marketing force. It happens at the point of maximum involvement, just when people are trying the product, just when they are making their most crucial decisions about the product: Will it work in my situation? Should I make a major commitment here? How should I interpret any negative experiences?

To summarize, what gives word of mouth most of its power is the fact that it is an experience-delivery mechanism. And it is successful experience that triggers full adoption behavior more than anything else.

Another way of saying this is that *lack of positive experience with a product is usually the single greatest factor holding it back from greater and faster acceptance.* The faster you deliver that experience, the faster people will feel comfortable enough to go to full adoption of your product.

A CASE IN POINT

Here's an example based on the type of actual cases that we'll look at in greater detail in Chapter 4. Let's say a new drug comes out which holds considerable promise for helping to alleviate the symptoms of a disease. Physicians read the studies and talk to the salespeople from the drug company. That's how they know the drug holds promise. But how do they know how it will work out in actual practice? They try it on a few patients who haven't responded well to existing drugs. These, of course, are the patients on whom the drug is least likely to be effective, but it is easiest to justify trial in these cases. Suppose that after trying a new drug on five of these refractory patients, one gets better, one stays the same, one gets worse, one has other possibly unrelated complications, and one moves to Florida. These results are uninterpretable, so physicians have to wait for five more patients in low-risk situations on whom to try the drug. This usually goes on for years, until enough word of mouth accumulates for physicians to be able to talk with each other and share success stories, tips, and suggestions for coping with problems, and other experiences. This expands the "experience pool" enough to enable physicians to form reliable opinions. Then, and only then—often after a few years have elapsed—the chain reaction reaches critical mass and explodes into enough word of mouth to cause the drug to go rapidly to full usage, sometimes in a matter of months.

The pattern of product acceptance seen in this example is similar for most business-to-business, industrial, high-tech, and professional products. It even holds true for many consumer products, especially those that are not easily tried or that are costly or risky to try. The time frame and other details may be different. But what is the same is the fact that it is the *time it takes to accu-*

mulate enough favorable experience—and to communicate that experience—to make a reasonable decision *that determines a product's success and the speed with which it is accepted.* It is the content, speed, and sources of word of mouth that mediate the process and act as the accelerator or the brake on the speed of adoption.

The quicker people can get experience under their belts, the quicker they will adopt the product. Word of mouth determines the speed of experience gathering. Therefore, word of mouth determines speed of product adoption.

Other Reasons Why Word of Mouth Is a Powerful Persuader

Even though you already know many if not most of the other reasons that word of mouth is so effective, seeing them all summarized in one place will probably make you realize why word of mouth is even more powerful than you think.

It's More Relevant and Complete

Word of mouth is "live," not canned like most company communication. When a friend tells you about a book, movie, or other product that she thinks you would like, she is telling you because she thinks that *you*—not some anonymous stranger—would like it. She wouldn't tell you about it if she thought you weren't interested in it. The point here is that word of mouth is *custom tailored* to the people who are participating in it. When someone recommends a product to a colleague, she isn't giving a pitch. She is responding to questions, the most important questions, the ones the decision makers themselves are asking. Therefore, customers pay more attention to it because it is perceived as *more relevant* and *more complete* than any other form of communication.

It's the Most Honest Medium

Because it is custom tailored, and because people are independent of the company, it is the most honest medium. And customers know it. Advertising and salespeople are notoriously biased and not fully truthful. The inherent honesty of word of mouth further adds to its credibility.

It's Customer Driven

Closely related to the two reasons given above, word of mouth is the most customer driven of all communications channels. The customer determines whom he will talk to, what he will ask, or whether he will continue to listen or politely change the subject.

It Feeds on Itself

Word of mouth is like a breeder reactor. It is *self-generating*, self-contained, and it wastes nothing. If ten people have ten experiences each, that's one hundred direct experiences. If they each tell ten people about their own experiences, that's an additional 1000 (indirect) experiences, which can be just as powerful as the direct experiences. If they each tell ten people, that's an additional 1000 people who now have 10,000 experiences in their heads. And so on. It's amazing how fast this accumulates. For instance, if 25 people tell 25 people and the process is repeated five more times, the number equals approximately the population of the United States. One more iteration, and the number equals approximately the population of the entire world!

It doesn't take long for everyone to hear about the wonders of the product, often several times each, which provides additional confirmation (e.g., "everybody's talking about it").

In contrast, an ad in a magazine may be seen by only the two or three people who read each copy, since the exposure is limited to just the direct and pass-along readers. Thus, to hit a lot of people you have to use mass media. Word of mouth is *unlimited*. In theory, you could tell just the right fountainhead influencer, she would tell ten, who would tell ten, who would tell ten, who would tell ten, who would tell ten, who would tell ten, who would tell ten, who would tell ten. That's 100 million hits! Most topical jokes make the rounds like this (yes, actually starting from one person!) in a matter of a day or two.

I call this *The Law of the Fountainhead Influencer*. Give me the one right person to start and I'll change the world. Of course, in real life, you would try to reach and convince dozens to hundreds of *leveraged influencers* (or just one Oprah), thereby increasing the chances of reaching the critical mass to sustain a word-of-mouth chain reaction and explosion.

Why are these fountainhead and leveraged influencers powerful enough to spark a chain reaction? Why don't they tell a few people about the product only to have the whole process peter out? Because they are luminaries, experts, gurus, and mavens. They each have a *sphere of influence* that may be worldwide, national, or local in nature. Their sphere of influence may number in the dozens up to the hundreds of millions. Oprah can sure move books.

These experts have one overriding attribute that gives them their influence: trust. People trust them to filter, distill, and objectively evaluate the overwhelming amount of information, make sense of it, and present it in a recommendation that is most likely to be right. We will see in Chapter 6 what the role of experts is versus peers in the decision process, but right now we just need to know that there are tiers of experts and influencers who tend to initiate word of mouth, sustain it, give it even more credibility, and supply the initial bang that can start the chain reaction of word of mouth.

For instance, I have several friends who like to discover new restaurants in the New York area. They read the columns of reviewers (one form of expert) who share their tastes, then fax my wife and me reviews of restaurants that seem to be worth going to. Often, they have already sampled the restaurant, so they can add a recommendation of their own. I know a few people who have never steered me wrong. So, when I need a restaurant in a particular area, I call them. They are my local influencers. The same process works with movies, novels, business books, computers, or cars.

This phenomenon of people liking to review things and engage in word of mouth is the entire basis of the phenomenally popular *Zagat* guides to restaurants and hotels. People rating restaurants is a way of formalizing and counting word-of-mouth recommendations. Also, the *Zagat* guides' popularity is almost entirely due to word of mouth from the people who use them. In other words, the *Zagat* guides are an example of the rare phenomenon of a word-of-mouth medium that is itself sold primarily by word of mouth (so-called viral marketing).

At this writing, the publishers are taking an interesting gamble by giving away their complete listings free on their Web site. If their hard copy books keep selling, they will probably continue to give away their ratings on the Web site. If they don't, they will probably charge or make the revenues through advertising. If they are as smart as I think they are, they will build in word-of-mouth components, such as a forum, as well as a simple way to get people to send ratings of recommended restaurants to their friends. For instance, make it "one-click simple" to invite friends to dinner, using the *Zagat* ratings: "Would you like to join me at Restaurant X (there actually is such a place, and it's great by the way)? Here is the Zagat description and rating. Click here to go to the Zagat site for the menu, driving directions, more Zagat ratings, or to suggest alternative restaurants." One could also add collaborative filtering, an amazing form of "electronic word of mouth" described in Chapter 7. All of this could drive people to the Web site and to the restaurants.

Word of Mouth Becomes One of the Product's Attributes

It's important to notice also that the recommendation by experts, whether an unsolicited testimonial or a paid endorsement, becomes part of the product's attributes. Your favorite movie star or director may come out with a new movie. That's one plus. But now if it's recommended by your favorite reviewers, *that becomes part of the product.* It's now "two thumbs up" by Roger Ebert and four stars by Leonard Maltin. These endorsements and testimonials may be even more important than who stars in the movie. Now if, in addition, three friends who share your tastes and who have successfully recommended movies you have liked in the past also loved it, you are going to see it. Notice that testimonials are a major part of most movie ads.

The important thing to remember here is that the "recommended by" becomes one of the product attributes, often the most important one.

Experts Like to Influence

It should be obvious by now that the *source* of the word of mouth is crucially important. But there are some consequences of the importance of the source that aren't so obvious:

One of the reasons that the initial stages of word of mouth are sustained and can spread so rapidly is that influencers like to influence. That's one of the reasons that they are influencers. If they didn't enjoy the process, they would keep their mouths shut and their keyboards still.

There are a variety of reasons why experts like to be experts that we needn't analyze here. Whatever the reasons in any particular case, they like to talk with each other (and almost always report that they don't get enough of it), they like to influence nonexperts, and they like to teach. There is more on this subject later.

Word of Mouth Saves Time and Money

Another attribute of word of mouth is that it can be extremely efficient. If you want to buy a product that you don't know too much about, the best way is often to find a few people who have investigated the product, and learn from them what they have found out.

For example, when I was looking for a supplier to put up my Web site, I decided to check with a colleague and friend whom I've known for thirty years. He has extremely high standards and is even more demanding than I am likely to be of this type of supplier. He told me he had found a supplier who would be willing to work along with customers who wanted to do new things. Since I was thinking about some innovative Web services, this is just what I was looking for.

To me it was a "no brainer." I called the supplier, verified the prices, and opened an account. I had my Web site up a few days later. So, a savvy friend with high standards had thoroughly investigated the market, and then had direct positive experience, saving me weeks of investigation (he had taken two weeks). I couldn't go too far wrong—I could always switch my domain name to a different supplier—and I was extremely unlikely to find anyone better.

The trick, of course, is to find the perfect advisor—we will explore this further in Chapter 6. What is important to understand now is that word of mouth can be an enormous time saver, even when it might appear to be very time consuming. For instance, you might have to fly to a conference, or attend a seminar, or hire a consultant to access word of mouth. These activities take more time than reading a few brochures, but the product literature gives you only promises. Word of mouth gives you reality.

It's a Mysterious, Invisible, Illusory Force

Like the radiation of a nuclear reaction, word of mouth is an invisible force (sometimes even called "underground" communication, or "the grapevine," or "the word," or "the buzz"). You see its effects all right, but not directly.

More than likely, you and your competitors think that sales are due to your (or your competitors') active promotional efforts. For instance, you take a bunch of actions, such as sending out a load of materials and ads launching a product. You see an effect in the marketplace. What could be more natural than to think that your action caused the effect? Actually, it is more than likely that your actions sparked a word-of-mouth chain reaction, and it was *the word of mouth that caused the effects* (see Figure 2-1).

Figure 2-1
What Causes Sales—Illusion versus Reality

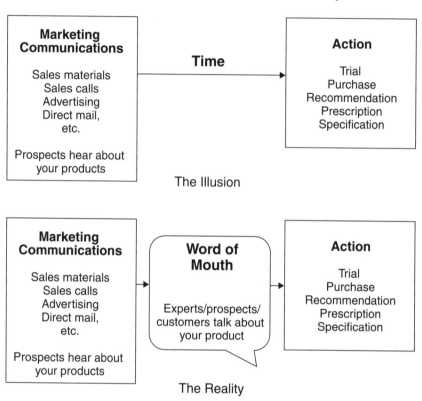

So, the illusion is that the advertising, or the sales message, or the mailing caused the effects. In fact, many products succeed *despite* the marketing supporting it, for reasons different from the positioning of the product or the most-emphasized benefits. If the advertising and sales force were aligned with the word of mouth, you could have had a much faster launch, at a much lower cost. It is what will go down the word-of-mouth channel—and be amplified by it—that should drive advertising and sales, not the other way around. This is a paradigm shift that will be explained further in Chapter 6.

To summarize the properties of word of mouth and the reasons for its power, word of mouth:

- Is the most powerful, influential, persuasive force in the marketplace (the most obvious reason)

- Is an experience-delivery mechanism (the most important and overlooked reason)

- Is independent, therefore credible

- Becomes part of the product itself

- Is custom-tailored, more relevant, and complete

- Is self-generating, self-breeding, grows exponentially, sometimes explosively

- Is unlimited in speed and scope

- Can originate from a single source, or a relatively small number of sources

- Is extremely dependent on the nature of the source

- Can be tremendously time-saving, efficient, and labor-saving

- Is often negative, but the negatives can actually be positive

- Can be very inexpensive to stimulate, amplify, and sustain

We have looked at the attributes, properties, and characteristics of word of mouth to see why it's so powerful. In order to harness it, we now need to be able to answer the following questions about word of mouth:

- What is the content of the word of mouth?

- Who is originating the word of mouth (its sources)?

- Who is receiving it?

- What are the channels through which it travels?

When we understand the answers to these questions, we'll be ready to look at how to trigger a controlled chain reaction: how to get it started, how to amplify it, how to channel it, and how to cause it to go in our direction.

Without understanding these four areas, my telling you how to trigger word of mouth will be like playing with nuclear power without knowing how to control it or how to take the appropriate safeguards. Without a clear understanding, it will either fizzle or blow up in your face.

CHAPTER 3

The Nine Levels of Word of Mouth

Of course, not all word of mouth is the same. There are several levels of word of mouth that are quite different from each other and that vary both in nature and intensity. The following section describes the nine levels of word of mouth, ranging from the "minus 4" level, where the talk about your product is only negative, to the "plus 4" level, where everyone is raving about the product.

Negative ◄————————————————► Positive

The Minus Levels
Minus 4

People are all talking about your product and complaining about it. It has reached to the level of public scandal. People are asking each other about it and actively dissuading other people from using it. If this is a short-term emergency, such as a product recall that is reacted to quickly and responsibly, the product can survive. Tampax, Tylenol, and Marv Albert come to mind. But if the scandal continues for any sustained length of time, the only way a product can survive is to be a needed product that has a monopoly, that creates an addiction, or that is so trusted that almost nothing can taint it.

The United States Postal Service (or indeed virtually any branch of government), managed health care, cigarettes, and heroin come to mind. Word of mouth is such a powerful force that almost nothing can withstand its onslaught. Observe that alternatives to the Postal Service grew up so rapidly that they threatened to put it out of business. In fact, if the Postal Service was not protected by the government, and if it had not made many recent improvements, it would have been long gone. You can safely predict that managed health care, in its present form, will also cease to exist. Virtually everybody, including the providers themselves, is actively complaining about the system as it is presently constructed. Nothing can survive such an onslaught of negative word of mouth when a viable alternative inevitably comes along.

Interestingly, humor can be a powerful form of negative word of mouth. The following two examples are probably apocryphal, but they will certainly illustrate how powerful word of mouth actually is,

A CASE IN POINT

Remember Ernestine the telephone operator? She was a character created by Lily Tomlin at the height of the AT&T monopoly. At that time AT&T, known as "The Phone Company," was extremely arrogant and almost totally unresponsive to its customers. It behaved very much like the Postal Service before the latter began to encounter competition and started to behave more like a business. Ernestine was the embodiment of these attitudes. She flaunted a whimsical, capricious abuse of power. Her favorite line was "We are the phone company and we are omnipotent." She would sniff disdainfully and say, "I just unplugged Cleveland." She was very funny because she hit a raw nerve so accurately.

People would repeat the latest antics of Ernestine around the water cooler the next day. AT&T became an object of derision. After watching Ernestine, people became even less tolerant in their dealings with the phone company. A climate of ridicule was established toward a specific embodiment of something that was so large, diffuse, and pervasive that it could not previously be a focused target. Prior to that, the breakup of AT&T was almost impossible to imagine. In fact, AT&T itself was almost impossible to imagine. It is possible that once breakup talk started, the attitudes that were surfaced and focused by Ernestine fueled the movement toward breaking up AT&T. Of course, I can't prove it. However, once you realize fully how powerful word of mouth is, you will realize that it is at least plausible.

A CASE IN POINT

Another example, even more outrageous than Ernestine, happened one night when a TV commercial aired showing a "Soviet Union fashion show." A model walked down the runway as an announcer said something like, "eveningvear." The dumpy model was wearing a nondescript gray something-or-other totally without shape or style. Another scene then showed her wearing exactly the same outfit, but with another prop, such as a beach ball, as the announcer said, "svimvear." This was repeated several more times. This was at a time when the Soviet Union had become a laughingstock. Even the liberals, who had previously regarded Soviet communism as a noble experiment, were realizing that the whole thing was not viable. The Soviet Ambassador to the United States protested vigorously the next day to the State Department. The reaction was so disproportionate that I remember thinking at the time that the Soviet Union was going to collapse. I even said that to several people, who clearly thought it was a bizarre prediction. Keep in mind, this was way before the breakup of the Soviet Union, when almost no one was predicting it. Did the Soviet fashion show commercial bring down the Soviet Union? Of course not. It was a symptom of a widespread perception that the Soviet Union was ludicrous. It was one powerful instance of a peculiar kind of word of mouth. The disproportionate protest that it triggered was a clear signal that the end was near. So, a minor event can embody and serve as a symbol of widespread—even worldwide—word of mouth.

Another, more current example: It will be almost impossible for the Firestone brand to survive its tire recall scandal.

Minus 3

Customers and ex-customers go out of their way to convince the other people not to use your product, but it hasn't reached scandal proportions. Similar to Level Minus 4, almost nothing can survive this level.

As this book goes to press, Verizon DSL service is in this category, with DSL Web site rating services, such as DSLreports.com flooded with complaints, which I can confirm from personal experience. (What I'm doing here is itself an example of level minus three, going out of my way to describe how bad they are.) By the time you read this, they will probably have solved their problems. But at this point, every time I tell someone that I have Verizon DSL service, they ask me whether I can keep my connection up and running. Of course, I can't, and everyone seems to know it.

Minus 2

When asked, customers rant, although they don't go out of their way to badmouth (isn't *that* an interesting phrase?) your product. They go on and on about how terrible your product is. Your product sales will slowly erode in this situation. The process will be slower because people are not actively seeking each other out to spread negative word of mouth.

However, paradoxically, the more ads or sales calls you make, *the faster your sales can erode* because of this negative word of mouth! This is because almost every time prospects get interested in your product, they will talk it over with someone else who will condemn it. Trying to put out word-of-mouth fires with conventional marketing only throws gasoline on the flames.

A good example of this level is Packrat, which was one of the best personal-information-management-software products on the market. However, it released its version 5 before working out some of the kinks. Its loyal customers, many of whom were participating in a forum on CompuServe, tried to help each other through the problems, but then quickly turned against the product when many of them felt that they were not being dealt with in a straightforward manner. They started asking each other what was the best product to switch to, and most of them decided it was a product called Ecco. Many switched, told their friends, and PackRat was virtually dead. Ecco assumed the dominant market position at the time, to be later followed by Outlook.

Minus 1

In this stage, people are not actively complaining about your product, but when they are asked, they have relatively negative things to say. Here, advertising and other conventional marketing can sometimes provide a holding action, but very little progress will be made. For example, most phone companies, particularly wireless companies, are in this category. People are usually mildly dissatisfied with the present state of wireless communication, but are not so angry that they go out of their way to badmouth their carrier. It's a great example of people buying something despite the negatives.

Level 0

At this level, people use your product, but are rarely asked about it. They don't volunteer their opinion. If asked, they have little (good or bad) to say about it. This is a product that is getting little or no word of mouth. It's probably going to cost a fortune to get such a product widely accepted. It's the level where most products are.

The Plus Levels
Plus 1

When asked, people have nice things to say about your product. For example, people may not necessarily go out of their way to tell anybody about a product or service from local merchants, such as dry cleaners or restaurants, but if asked, they'll say it's good, reliable, or any of the other nice things that are true about the product. This is already a cut above the word-of-mouth level of most products.

In this situation, conventional marketing can trigger massive word of mouth if it can get people to the next level, Plus 2.

Plus 2

When asked, customers rave. They go on and on about how wonderful your product is. Here, conventional marketing is almost completely wasted because it is so much less powerful than what is sitting there for the taking. What is needed is for you to provide the channels and materials for your customers to rave. An example, as of this writing, is the Pocket PC. It needs to get to the next level, which people will be motivated to make happen, so that more compatible software and e-books can be generated.

Plus 3

At this level, customers go out of their way to convince other people to use your product. This is what people talk about at parties: the new movie, the latest restaurant, the latest book. (You will talk about *this* book at your next business gathering, won't you?) Again, provide the encouragement and the channels, facilitate the process, and build a bigger plant.

Plus 4

Your product is being talked about continually. People are asking each other about it. Experts, local influencers, typical customers, and prospects are all talking with each other about your product or service and raving about its virtues. It is getting a considerable amount of publicity.

At this level, it is especially necessary to manage people's expectations. Otherwise, people will expect much more than will be delivered, which is a sure recipe for disappointment. In this kind of a situation, sales are often growing at such a rapid rate that the company cannot maintain quality. Again, expectations must be managed.

"Plus 4" Companies: The following are examples of companies representing different industries that have reaped the benefit of level "Plus 4" word of mouth.

> *Lexus Automobiles:* Lexus regularly conducts open houses of its customers. During a recall, they contacted each customer individually and arranged to fix the car in the customer's driveway or the parking lot of the customer's business. Lexus has an extraordinary customer satisfaction program that directly causes word of mouth. It includes sending multipage questionnaires to its customers, which not only assess customer satisfaction, but also lead customers to the awareness of how satisfied they are. But the word of mouth that I've been hearing lately is that their dealers are undoing much of what the company has created. I got rid of my Lexus mostly because of dealer dissatisfaction.
>
> If you think that only a high profit, luxury car company can afford such a customer satisfaction program, then how do you explain Saturn?
>
> *The Saturn Car Company:* Saturn has a car club, and the way the company has built its customers into a "family" is nothing short of miraculous. Saturn even conducts a nationwide bar-

becue for all of its customers, some of whom drive thousands of miles not to miss it. What do they talk about? Among other things, how much they love their cars.

Harley-Davidson: Harley conducts events around the country, often with the company's top executives attending, of course on their own "Hogs."

Netscape Navigator: Built entirely upon word of mouth, Netscape captured about 90 percent of the Web browser market before it placed its first ad. The company did it by giving away the first versions of its product, and by word of mouth, primarily on the Internet. Netscape has now been overtaken by Internet Explorer.

Celestial Seasonings Herbal Tea: During its first years, the company's president, Mo Siegel, enclosed a note in each box of tea. His message was that it was a small company that could not afford to advertise. He asked that people tell their friends about his wonderful herbal teas or, better yet, to serve it to their friends. He said, "We have spent all kinds of money on fancy advertising, but all of our marketing research shows that the most important driver of our business is word of mouth, particularly word of mouth about our packaging."

The Internet: The Internet is probably the most important communications advance in human history—arguably even more important than the printing press, whose the products (books) could be used only by the elite until relatively recent times. The Internet took off almost entirely on its own through word of mouth. It is a truly democratic phenomenon, owned and controlled by no one entity. It took off with no marketing, just people telling people, telling people.

Apple Computer: Apple, whose customers became almost a cult, is another example of companies—like Noxzema and

Hershey—that did not advertise until relatively late in the game and relied almost entirely on word of mouth in the form of dealer recommendations and friends telling friends.

Word of Mouth in the Real World

For a glimpse into how word of mouth can work in the real world, consider the following two examples. The first is an article about that appeared in the *Wall Street Journal* on November 8, 1996.

A CASE IN POINT

THE SNOW-EASE SHOVEL

The Front Lines
by Thomas Petzinger, Jr.
Penny Nirider Has an Unusual View: She Likes Her Customers
Thorntown, Indiana

Her success sprang from a blizzard, a football game and a talk show. But mostly it came from her instinct for putting herself in her customers' shoes.

Penny Nirider, 36 years old, is a whiz with a spreadsheet. Even in this town of 3,000, she found plenty of work helping companies computerize accounts. Because she had two small boys she worked from her home, usually between 9 p.m. and 2 a.m.

About three years ago, with the boys starting school, she took a day job handling accounts payable for a company called Enduron. Enduron employed fifty-five people bending metal for Indiana's bustling travel-trailer industry. Automating the company made a huge difference on the bottom line, prompting the owners eventually to make Ms. Nirider a partner.

Metal-bending is a volatile business, so the company decided to diversify by purchasing a little plastics shop called Wilmarc. With just five employees, Wilmarc made composting bins, leaf baggers and an unusual rounded shovel that scraped away snow without bending or lifting. They called it Snow-Ease.

Ms. Nirider, given charge of the unit, discovered that running a small plastics business was nothing like running a spreadsheet. Wilmarc sold to hardware distributors, an industry she knew nothing about. There were no uniform sales agreements. She also sensed some hardware people didn't take her seriously because she was female.

Then, one day shortly before last Christmas, an elderly woman phoned Wilmarc headquarters. The caller owned a Snow-Ease but wanted another and couldn't find one. Would the factory ship her one?

Wilmarc had never sold directly to a customer. Indeed, each Snow-Ease folded into a feeble box designed for retail display, and Wilmarc shipped these strictly by the case. For all Ms. Nirider knew, distribution agreements prohibited selling at retail. But the caller was so sweet and seemed so needful! So a Snow-Ease carton was dispatched to Pittsburgh for $19.95, or $10 below retail.

Just after Christmas, the Big Snow hit the East. Lynn Cullen, the host of a popular AM talk show on Pittsburgh's WTAE, told her listeners that some miscreant had stolen her snow shovel. Later, off the air, Ms. Cullen heard from the elderly woman, who said she could solve her snow woes with a call to Indiana. When the call came, Ms. Nirider again could not say no.

A few days later, an employee named Monica Taylor opened up the cinder-block office here to find the phone already ringing. It was a third Pittsburgher seeking a Snow-Ease. The instant she hung up. Another call came in, also from Pittsburgh, then another and another. It was a stunt, she figured; the Pittsburgh Steelers were facing the Indianapolis Colts a week later in the playoffs. But soon it became obvious that the Pittsburgh radio personality was raving about the Snow-Ease and had given out Wilmarc's number over the air.

Unfortunately, she had also said the Snow-Ease sold for just $19.95.

Ms. Nirider agonized. Shipping boxes one at a time would be unprofitable and might upset distributors. But the Pittsburgh callers were buried in snow. And whoever was at fault for the price confusion, it certainly wasn't them.

"We didn't have a clue what we were doing," Ms. Nirider says. "But I knew what I would expect as a customer." So $19.95 it was.

There was yet another dilemma. Never having sold at retail, Wilmarc wasn't a credit-card merchant. But in a snow emergency, how could the company expect people to pay in advance? So Ms. Nirider shipped the product with invoices to follow. "It was just common courtesy," she says. (Barely 1 percent defaulted.)

As the orders rolled in, Ms. Nirider realized she was having more fun than she had ever enjoyed in business. Partly it was the escalating banter with callers over the approaching Colts-Steelers game. (The Steelers won, forcing Ms. Nirider to pay up on a few long-distance bets.) Everybody was so easygoing. Her gender, moreover, didn't matter. Dealing with the public, she found, "You get to be yourself. You don't have to play any games."

Unhappily, of course, the more she sold, the more she lost. With orders unabating after two weeks, she needed an honorable way out. So Wilmarc purchased ads on WTAE notifying people that several days hence, on Jan. 31, 1996, the company would begin charging the established retail price of $29.95.

Even at that price the orders flew in. Ms. Nirider noticed that many were soon coming from Ohio and West Virginia, thanks to *word of mouth* [emphasis mine]. By April, Wilmarc had sold 2,100 Snow-Ease shovels directly to consumers across the region, many times the number it sold through the usual distributors, none of whom complained.

Today, Wilmarc has a separate retail mail-order business. Ms. Nirider was hoping for 6,000 retail Snow-Ease orders [the winter of the *Wall Street Journal* article]. If word-of-mouth continues to multiply at the rate of last year, she figures the Snow-Ease may one day be ready for national promotion. [As of this writing, it is.]

> So if you ever see an advertisement for the Snow-Ease, I hope you'll recall the lesson of Penny Nirider: Every person who contacts your business—every elderly lady, every talk show host, every football fan—stands at the beginning of a long line of potential customers. Resolve dilemmas in their favor and they'll return [via word of mouth] to you more than you had to give away.

Notice how word of mouth has a way of crossing into the media, which in turn creates more one-to-one word of mouth. If it weren't an excellent and different product, the lady would not have called the radio station. But if only the people who heard the report on the radio bought the product, there would have been a small return. People told their friends (more word of mouth in the chain), so the orders came in for an extended period of time. Then the *Wall Street Journal* picked it up, which meant exponentially more word of mouth, as many thousands of people clipped it, discussed it, or acted directly on the information. Many other newspapers, publications, and broadcast interview shows that use newspapers like the *Wall Street Journal* as a source of their ideas picked up the story. More word of mouth. The article will have an extended life on the Internet. It is being reprinted in my book.

If this company handles things right, it will be a major product until some large company buys it and decides that it can't rely on only word of mouth. It will probably try to dramatize product's uniqueness, its benefits and features, in some artificial way, with actors, instead of putting that original elderly lady into the ads. It probably will not use the original radio personality, because "No one ever heard of her," despite the fact that she can obviously sell snow shovels. It will probably abandon the word-of-mouth mechanisms and channels that worked, in favor of less powerful media that it is more familiar with. In a subsequent interview with Penny Nirider, she did say that Wilmarc spent a load of money on advertising with no effect. It is still selling strongly through word of mouth. (P.S. You can find out more about the Snow-Ease shovel at www.snowease.com.)

A CASE IN POINT

POINT: TRIVIAL PURSUIT

In the early 1980s, Trivial Pursuit was an obscure Canadian board game. The late Linda Pezzano, a marketing consultant, forever changed the way makers of games market their products. It seems obvious now, but not then. And while it seems obvious, most people who read this will nod, think it obvious, and then skip over it without applying it to their business. Who is going to use these ideas, you or your competitors?

Pezzano sent the top buyers of toys a series of provocative messages months before the 1983 New York Toy Fair. She sent the game to Hollywood stars, such as Larry Hagman, Pat Boone, and Gregory Peck, and other people whose names were mentioned in its trivia questions. Many of these stars wrote letters of thanks, which she used in promotions. She staged tournaments every place she could, including bars, restaurants, clubs, and parks. Her campaign cost a fraction of what it cost her competitors, who engaged in traditional (for the toy business) marketing: They advertised on TV, got their games into movies, and made licensing agreements. Her word-of-mouth model is one that everyone now uses. By giving away a few hundred games at $12 wholesale cost, she started a fad and forever changed the way a whole industry markets. Does this, or part of this, or some transformed version of this, apply to your area?

Increasingly, smaller companies with superior products win against their larger competitors through the effective use of word of mouth. This is especially true today, given the widespread means for the dissemination of word of mouth, including e-mail, teleconferencing, online communications, and personal wireless phones. As the communications revolution progresses, it provides the infrastructure for the Word-of-Mouth Revolution.

CHAPTER 4

Harnessing Word of Mouth

Harnessing word of mouth is a process that consists of six steps.

The Six-Step Process

1. Figure out why someone should buy your product, given his or her values and priorities.

2. Identify the predominant adopter types that you need to be going after—innovators, early adopters, middle majority, late adopters, laggards—in your various markets.

3. Identify the crucial Decision Stages needed to adopt your product.

4. Combine 2 and 3 above, using the Decision Matrix™, to identify the content—the actual words, the word of mouth—that you will need to accelerate each problematic step. Both the decision process and the Decision Matrix are discussed in Chapter 5.

5. Identify, design and create the sources and delivery mechanisms of word of mouth that will be most per-

suasive and motivating. The sources are discussed in Chapter 6.

6. Create and implement the word-of-mouth campaign.

The six-step process can best be explained through an example.

A CASE IN POINT

Market Navigation once worked with a drug that was selling very well, but our client believed was selling at only a fraction of its potential. It had a strong warning about possible side effects that were based on some laboratory rat studies, but which had never been observed in humans even though it had been used millions of times throughout the world.

Step 1: Identify Why They Should Adopt

After conducting a series of focus groups, we determined that physicians had no doubt about the drug's efficacy and that most had tried it successfully. In fact, the more knowledgeable ones were extremely eager to prescribe it more aggressively, but were worried about the warning. It became clear that they were looking for justification to use it.

Step 2: Identify Adopter Types

But the middle majority was holding back. They were asking for long-range studies that would take years to conduct. Even if these studies were conducted, the suspicion would remain, since it's difficult to dislodge a negative impression.

Step 3: Identify the Crucial Decision Steps

The bottleneck was in going from trial to implementation. The drug worked, but the critical step was to provide *credible* assurances that it was safe.

Step 4: Identify the Actual Words They Would Need to Hear

Physicians needed to hear that it would be safe in their hands, in their situation, with their kinds of patients. They also needed to hear exactly why they would be on safe ground if they were sued for damages resulting from the use of this drug.

Step 5: Identify the Most Motivating Word-of-Mouth Sources

We found out that the most respected experts of the specialty involved were extremely favorable toward the drug. Even the next tier of leaders were favorable, and many were using it. We verified that this was a situation where physicians were willing to listen to the practical suggestions of the experts.

Step 6: Create and Implement the Word-of-Mouth Campaign

Among the various word-of-mouth elements was a teleconferenced seminar program that coincided with some compelling new uses of the drug. In these sessions, experts talked about: how to use it, the dubious science upon which the warnings were based, the fact that there were no cases worldwide of what they were concerned about, and the studies that they could cite to justify its use. They also expressed the opinion that physicians were doing much more harm by not using the drug more widely. We focused on all of the things that would give physicians the justification to use what our research told us they needed. After a relatively small number of sessions, concentrated on the opinion leaders of each major city, the use of the drug increased about twelvefold, making it one of the top three best-selling drugs in the country at the time.

The point of the above example is that this was a carefully constructed program, involving extensive word-of-mouth research, followed by a program that covered absolutely everything the physicians needed to accelerate their decisions. Leave one thing out, and the word of mouth goes nowhere.

Interestingly, the client was not sure that our program was the major factor in the sales increase. After all, the client was conducting many other promotion programs. It didn't look to any of us that such a simple, focused program could have made such a large difference, even if every physician in our program switched to our client's drug exclusively. It caused us to look back at past programs and discover the pattern of multifold increases mentioned before. It also caused us to analyze the underlying dynamics and mathematics of word of mouth. What we had failed to account for was the second-order effects of word of mouth, which are more powerful than the primary effects. Second-order effects mean that colleagues tell colleagues, who tell more colleagues, and so on. The word spreads at an ever-increasing pace until it reaches critical mass, and everyone is talking about it.

Put simply, conventional marketing proceeds at an arithmetic pace. Repeated exposures and hits cause people to gradually get more curious, informed, and comfortable. People then begin to desire the product. On the other hand, word of mouth, when it gets going, proceeds not at an *arithmetic* pace, not at a *geometric* pace, not at a *logarithmic* pace, but at an *exponential* pace more characteristic of an explosion than of a tortoise and hare race. It can quickly blast through all resistance, allowing people to give up part of their personal and laborious information search. It can also trigger the pent-up demand, as in the case above. It only takes one rock to start an avalanche.

In summary, you need to be brutally honest with yourself about the actual and perceived merits of your product, then figure out precisely—with as much rigor as you would construct an ad, mailing, or sales campaign—what the customer needs to hear from word of mouth, and what kind of word of mouth (e.g., from experts or peers). Then, you need to create situations and events that will cause the word of mouth to start, then spread like a wildfire, or explode like a nuclear reaction. Everything in the rest of your marketing should fan the flames.

The Process in Detail

1. *Figure out why someone should buy your product, given his or her values and priorities.*

   This is pretty much standard for sophisticated marketing. Look at things from your customers' point of view and figure out why each market segment should buy your product over your competition's. If you can't, you are not ready for a word-of-mouth program. You need to do additional work on the product and/or the offering.

2. *Identify the predominant adopter type(s) that you need to be going after—innovator, early adopter, middle majority, late adopter, laggard—in your various markets.*

   Each of your markets will have a predominant adopter type, given where you are in the product life cycle. (The adoption cycle will be discussed in greater detail in Chapter 5.) A recently launched product will be aimed at the innovators and the early adopters. At some point the leap must be taken to the middle majority, then the late adopters. Identify and concentrate where your efforts need to be. For instance, don't waste time going after the large, tempting, lucrative middle majority before you have made substantial headway with the early adopters, because it is the early adopters that the middle majority look to in order to confirm that the product works.

3. *Identify the crucial decision stages needed to adopt your product.*

   Map out the stages that a person will have to go through in order to make the decision to try and adopt your product. What will get them to engage in the decision process? What information will they need? What will they have to learn or be convinced of in order to further their decision?

The decision process is really a series of stages that lead up to full adoption. Usually one or several of these stages will constitute bottlenecks. If there were no bottlenecks, your product would be soaring and your factory would have trouble keeping up with the demand.

Identify the stages that word of mouth can handle best. For instance, the information about your product may be best handled by direct mail, or by salespeople. But confirming that your product really works and is safe in a certain kind of situation may be able to be handled only by direct experience—which the customer is reluctant to risk—or more safely by word of mouth.

4. *Combine steps 2 and 3 above, using the Decision Matrix™ (explained in Chapter 5) to identify the content—the actual words, the word of mouth—that you will need to accelerate each problematic step.*
   Each kind of adopter goes through a different set of steps to arrive at a decision. You need to gear your program to address the exact concerns of the adopter type and the particular stage this type is going to get stuck on.

   The Decision Matrix is a chart of the kinds of concerns that the different types of adopters have at different stages of the decision process and the specific word-of-mouth content that these people need to hear and that you need to stimulate in order to convince them to take the next steps. It's the result of over thirty years of experience.

5. *Identify, design, and create the sources and delivery mechanisms of word of mouth that will be most persuasive and motivating.*
   Now that you have identified precisely what the communications need to be, construct programs that address pre-

cisely the issues that you have identified. Construct the program in a focused way to zero in on exactly what will do the most to accelerate favorable decisions about the product among the widest number of people.

6. *Create and implement the word-of-mouth campaign.*
Make sure that all steps of the decision process are handled for all types of adopters, with the media that are most able to do the job right. For instance, advertising may create awareness among the largest number of people fastest, but salespeople may be able to qualify the people who are ready to buy and tailor the message to the right people. Incorporate exactly the word-of-mouth elements into all media that are most needed, such as *verifiably persuasive* studies quoted in ads, or references to local opinion leaders' usage by the salespeople.

But little will happen until you take the next step: Create the events that will directly spread word of mouth to confirm and verify that the claims are true, that it works in the customer's situation, and that it is otherwise OK to use the product. We'll see how later.

Craft the word-of-mouth campaign in a variety of media because different people have different preferences, ranging from live meetings, teleconferences, networking events, packaged audio tapes, and video tapes to web sites and discussion groups.

Choreograph all of these elements to accelerate your prospects through their decision process.

Thirty Ways of Harnessing Word of Mouth

Subsequent chapters provide expanded descriptions and tips, but use this list as a summary checklist:

Using Experts

❑ Advisory groups

   ❑ Customers

   ❑ Suppliers

   ❑ Experts

   ❑ Salespeople

❑ Experts' roundtables

❑ Experts' selling groups

Seminars, Workshops, and Speeches

❑ Speakers program

❑ Seminars

❑ Group selling

❑ Dinner meetings

❑ Peer selling groups

❑ Teleconferenced experts' panels

❑ Trade show events/opportunities

"Canned" Word of Mouth

❑ Videotapes

❑ Audiotapes

❑ World Wide Web

❑ CDs

Referral Selling

❑ Testimonials

❏ Networking

❏ Referral selling program

"New" Media

❏ Hotlines

❏ Faxback services

❏ Web-based word of mouth, forums, e-mail, etc.

❏ Call centers

Using Traditional Media for Word of Mouth

❏ Customer service as a word-of-mouth engine.

❏ PR

❏ Placements

❏ Events

❏ Promotions

❏ Word of mouth in ads, sales brochures, or direct mail

❏ Salesperson programs, such as sales stars, peer training, or using salespeople as word-of-mouth generators

❏ Word-of-mouth incentive programs ("tell-a-friend" programs

❏ Useful gifts to customers (such as articles, how-to manuals) that they can give to their friends

Internal Word of Mouth

Every employee of your company should be actively spreading word of mouth about your products.

When people inside your company tell their friends "inside information," it is particularly credible. When they tell their friends that the obsession with quality you are advertising is actually true, people tend to believe them. Even though they might be employees of the company, they are not paid spokespeople. They have no particular reason to be telling you these things unless they are true. In fact, many people tend to complain about the companies in which they work. So, when employees of a company express great enthusiasm about it and its products, they are extremely persuasive.

How do you get this going? It takes many years to build up the kind of employee attitudes that are widespread at Procter & Gamble, Merck, and Microsoft. You have to demonstrate values at the top that become pervasive throughout the organization. Frankly, most companies don't have these attitudes and will never get their employees to wage a positive word-of-mouth campaign on their behalf.

Mission statements have been popular for some time now. However, most people recognize that these statements are just empty words unless they are lived every day, particularly by top management who set the example.

Some corporate cultures are more fertile grounds for internal word of mouth than others. In a company that has the right conditions — meaning a company that is genuinely outstanding, that has a strong sense of ethics, and that treats its people like people — internal word of mouth can be a very powerful tool.

How to Spur Internal Word of Mouth

- First of all, ask for it. Ask people to pass the word about important company news and product developments.

- Find every example of what you want to promote, such as superior customer service, and spread the stories, since word of mouth tends to be spread by stories.

- Give people a common mission and make their rewards dependent upon the accomplishment of that mission.

- Most of all, give internal word of mouth the attention that it deserves. Research it, and make it a priority. You can find some suggestions on how to research employee word of mouth in Appendix C.

CHAPTER 5

Using Word of Mouth to Speed the Decision Process

A large number of your prospects and customers are meeting significant blocks in the decision process. If not, each and every one of them would be fully committed, enthusiastic, evangelistic, repeat customers. I can't name a single product—and certainly not a company—that fully fits this description. It's an ideal that probably no product will ever fully reach.

It's important to examine the blocks and friction points that keep prospects from becoming customers—and customers from becoming raving fans—and the critical role word of mouth can play in smoothing out those transitions. As we have seen, word of mouth alone can be sufficient to move prospects into buying mode. In the course of hearing thousands of word-of-mouth discussions on hundreds of products, certain patterns of decision making have emerged. Almost all marketers think of their industry as specialized, and think of their product and customers as unique. They are right. But underneath the profound differences in products, customers, and industries, there is an underlying structure to how word of mouth influences the decision process.

By understanding this structure and adding the uniqueness of your industry, you can encourage the word of mouth that will be most effective with each type of customer at each stage of the decision process. If your customers are primarily at one particular stage of the decision process, you can concentrate on encouraging the type of word of mouth that will have the most impact on their decision.

The Decision Process

The decision process takes place in five broad stages:

> **Stage 1. *Deciding to decide.*** Going from disinterested status quo to active investigation.

> **Stage 2. *Selecting among options:***
>   **a.** Identifying options
>   **b.** Studying options
>   **c.** Weighing options

> **Stage 3. *Trial:*** Observing the product in use and evaluating its performance.

> **Stage 4. *Purchase/Implementation/Ongoing usage.*** Becoming a customer.

> **Stage 5. *Expanding use and recommending.*** Moving beyond intended use and becoming a product advocate.

Your job as a marketer is to sell your product by helping people move from status quo to stage 5. Before we consider each of the five stages in detail, let's look at the state of mind of customers when they are in the predecision, or status quo, stage.

Predecision: The Status Quo, or "Ignorance Is Bliss," Stage

There is an old saying that "ignorance is bliss." I don't know where it comes from, and I have never met anyone who really believes it. But in the world of marketing, customers act *as if* they believe it. They act as if they prefer to be ignorant. Why?

In this age of information overload, when people are faced with relatively low priority information, they choose not to process it. They don't have the time, resources, and tolerance of uncertainty to look at new products, unless those products are potentially vital to their lives.

You might have the greatest product that ever came along, but you have first to get the attention and *active* interest of your target. Otherwise, your product will be largely ignored.

Most prospects are unwilling to take in relatively low priority new knowledge.

Nowadays, people most often buy products that will *substantially* save time or reduce effort. If saving time and effort *in the decision process* is part of the mix, so much the better. It is word of mouth that can cut through the information overload.

The information and communications revolution has caused another problem, closely related to the overload already mentioned. If the glut of information threatens to monopolize all available time, it also challenges each discrete message to get noticed. In marketing circles, that challenge is called clutter, or noise. Even if you had the right message, how are you going to get heard above the din?

Your prospect is practically buried under an avalanche of communication, besieged by deadlines, in a downsized corporation or rapidly expanding company (or both), without assistance, worried about being "rightsized" (fired), or worried about doing the work of six people. *This person couldn't care less about listening to you.* Yes, even you, with just the right product for her. This person may want a better widget, but she has no interest in a deliberative decision-making process that entails a learning curve. What she really wants is some peace and quiet, or anything approaching a feeling of control, or a little fun.

That is the status quo. That's the situation that your customer starts out in. That's the situation you are trying to enter when you come knocking at her door, or luring her to your Web site.

Stage 1. Deciding to Decide

First, let me tell you how you *don't* get through. You *don't* join the frenzy. There are enough frantic Web sites, brochures, ads, and commercials. They rarely work. Don't believe the less creative ad agencies that tell you that you have to get through by brute force, that you have to make enough noise (noise? I thought they were in the communication business!), or be more "intrusive." No kidding, "intrusive" is actually the word they use.

Nevertheless, separating your message from the clamor is crucial. You need to make a surgical strike: a claim or promise so penetrating, exciting, and relevant that it gets through the filter most people have to keep information out. The main purpose of a filter is not to keep things out, but—a fact usually overlooked—to let the right things in.

How do you come up with the right claim or promise? You listen to the word of mouth, to what customers say in individual interviews and in focus groups. You have to be careful because people rarely communicate directly. You need to try out a lot of different approaches and see what turns people on about your product.

One thing is for sure: It's almost always going to be something different from what you think it is. The customer's perspective is different from yours.

It's important to realize that customers are not at this point making a decision about your product. They are making a decision about *whether to even pay attention to your claims.*

But you don't want only their attention. A clown can get their attention. And you don't want only their interest. A cute kid, an animal, or a celebrity sex symbol can get their momentary interest. You want them to be *receptive and involved,* actively interested in what you have to say about what your product can do for them.

There is only one way to do that: *Make them a credible promise to give them information about how to get something that they strongly want.* And the best way to get that promise listened to is to get it delivered by word of mouth from other people. We'll get to *how* later, after we understand more about the steps of the decision process and the different types of customers we are trying to influence.

The kind of word of mouth that moves people at this stage of the decision process centers around the claim, the promise, and the expected benefits. It's all about possibilities, hopes, and dreams:

- "You really ought to find out about the Internet because…"

- "Have you heard of X? You really ought to look into it."

- "What? You don't have a laptop, a Palm®, a Rio® (or whatever the current electronic must-have is)? How do you live without it?"

- "You live there and don't have a four-wheel drive? Wow!"

- "What's your e-mail address? What? How come you don't have one?|

- "Did you hear that Professor A at Harvard says that any doctor who isn't using X is practically committing malpractice?"

The real main message of this type of word of mouth, at this stage of the decision process, is "You'd better pay attention to this new development" rather than "This is the product to buy."

Stage 2. Selecting among Options

Your prospect is interested in either your product category ("I'm in the market for a new computer") or your product. Most people will not go ahead and act without doing three things:

1. Identifying other options

2. Studying information about these options

3. Judging which of these options is most likely to deliver the expected benefits in their situation

People often find out about the existence of other options from experts (for instance, in industry magazines, such as *Consumer Reports*), then get information from trusted advisors (for instance, from dealers), and then find out what is working— from peers who are in similar situations. It's important to understand what the various sources of word of mouth do, something we'll examine in Chapter 6. Right now, you need to understand that, at this stage of the decision process, a lot is going on. The simplest way to think of it is as one stage with three parts: identifying, studying, and weighing options.

Word of mouth that moves people at this stage centers around "hard" information:

1. Finding options
   - ■ "There are several possibilities in your situation."
   - ■ "Have you looked at X? They have a great selection."

2. Studying options (gathering information about options)
   - ■ "Here's some information about the product, but what's really important is ...."

- "Here's what really seems to be working out best for most people...."

3. Weighing options

- "I've been using it in a situation like yours. What works out best for me is...."

- "This product is the best in most circumstances, but not in yours...."

- "The negatives the company and its salespeople aren't talking about are...."

- "Here's the lowdown about the problems.... But here's how to avoid them."

- "The product looks good on paper, but in the real world...."

Stage 3. Trial

Once the prospect has decided which of the options is most likely to be the best for him, he needs to confirm that the information is true, and verify that it will in fact work out as anticipated in his situation.

There is only one thing that will accomplish this: experience. There are only two ways to get experience: directly or indirectly.

Direct Experience Isn't Always the Best Teacher. Although direct experience has the advantage that it is gathered in the actual situation in which the product will be used, it does have many disadvantages:

- When you try a product, you are inexperienced (that's why you're trying to get experience!). You are likely to use the product in an unskilled manner and have negative experiences with it. Of course, this applies not only to sophisticated products such as electronics. Even buying a new car —or even simpler products—can be stressful for most people.

■ These negative experiences are often risky, costly, or damaging to self-esteem and reputation.

■ It is time consuming to try new products.

■ Trying new products yourself can be very unsettling, confusing, disconcerting, embarrassing, and anxiety producing. Many people shun the uncertainty and ambiguity inherent in a direct trial, especially of a new product.

Entrepreneurs, teachers, and many marketers have absolutely no apparent appreciation of or tolerance for this mentality.

Indirect Experience Is Often Preferred. Fortunately, there's indirect or vicarious experience to the rescue. A product doesn't have to be tried directly by the prospect, nor does it have to be tried in the exact situation in which it will ultimately be used. People can attend a demonstration, make a site visit, or find some other way of observing the product in action. But the best source of indirect experience is word of mouth: talking with people who are using the product and getting their reactions. That way your prospects can learn from someone else's experience instead of learning in the school of hard knocks.

Indirect experience can be better in many ways than direct experience, despite the fact that it doesn't take place in the exact situation in which the prospect will use the product.

■ It's safer. For instance, a doctor is—in effect—trying out a new drug on some other doctors' patients!

■ It provides a larger sample and a broader range of experience: Prospects can talk with more people and get the benefit of more uses of the product than would be likely directly.

- It is less costly, less time consuming, and less visible.

- Mistakes aren't your prospect's mistakes. She can't get in trouble, can't be embarrassed, can't look foolish, etc.

- Your prospect can learn from other people's mistakes.

If your prospect observes and talks with people for whom the product worked and who may be less skilled or less intelligent than he is, then he can be pretty sure the product will work even better in his hands.

Word of mouth that moves people at this stage centers around *experience.*

The Actual Trial

- "How have you found the product to perform?"

- "Had any trouble with it?"

- "What's the safest way to try it?"

- "This product really exceeds my expectations."

- "Wow! Was I surprised when I tried X."

- "Try it, you'll like it."

- "I was more skeptical than you were, but I tried it and liked it."

Stage 4: Purchase, Implementation, and Ongoing Usage

Once the trial has been successful, the prospect has to inform others of her intention to implement use of the product. She has to deal with announcements, availability, delivery, service, guarantees, and training issues. In some cases, she has to decide where the product fits in with other alternative products.

At this stage, the word of mouth that moves people centers around practicality of implementation.

- "It really was a smooth transition."

- "It didn't disrupt my operation."

- "It was easy for my people to learn."

- "There was a minor problem that they fixed immediately."

- "My people welcomed it."

Stage 5: Expanding Use and Recommending

Here is where the customer moves from a person who has implemented the product, to full usage, and—ultimately—to full adoption. I call this "full rational usage." Most products are not one-shot deals but are used over and over again. Even when someone is a "customer," he still has a choice of whether to use your product as his product of first, second, or third choice. He still has a choice of how frequently to use your product. He still has choices of new circumstances in which to use your product. So, priority, frequency, and new uses can be as important as brand choice.

A good example of this issue was the slogan, "Reach for the Campbell's. It's right on your shelf." It was determined that most people had Campbell's soup on their shelves; they just didn't think to use it frequently enough.

Avon's Skin So Soft is an example of using an established product differently and strongly recommending it: It was a modestly selling skin softener whose sales went through the roof when people recommended it to their friends as a benign insect repellent, despite the company's initial claims that it had no insect-repellent activity whatsoever!

Once a person feels comfortable regularly using your product, she will want to recommend it both as a self-justification and so that other people will benefit from the product.

The kind of word of mouth that moves people at this stage centers around new and expanded usage:

- ◼ "I'm using it all the time."

- ◼ "Have you tried it for X?"

- ◼ "I don't know how I could live without it."

- ◼ "I really think you should try it."

- ◼ "I recommend it highly."

How Word of Mouth Works in Different Parts of the Adoption Cycle

We have seen that a different kind of word of mouth is effective at *different stages* of the decision process. Word of mouth also affects people differently, depending on where they are in the *adoption cycle.* It is essential that you understand this, because if you don't encourage the right kind of word of mouth for each kind of adopter and tailor it to where the individual is in the decision process, you will be hitting people with the wrong messages and turning them off.

The adoption cycle is usually broken down into five kinds of people:

1. Innovators

2. Early adopters

3. Middle majority

4. Late adopters

5. Laggards

These five "types" describe how people break out into recognizable patterns when faced with a decision in the marketplace. Identifying targets in this very specific way narrows down what word-of-mouth message they will respond to most strongly.

The *innovator* wants to hear from experts that *the product is unique, technologically advanced, and cutting-edge.* This kind of person wants to stand out from the crowd and to be ahead of the pack—in a word, "*outstanding.*"

The *early adopter* tends to be a visionary, who sees the *possibilities* to which the product would apply. This person wants to hear word of mouth about the power of the product and is willing to take chances on it for its potential advantages. This person is driven by a desire to be *excellent.*

The *middle majority* tends to be people who are most concerned with the *practicalities* of applying the product. These people definitely do not want to be the first to try a product. But they also don't want to be the last. They agree with Alexander Pope in his *An Essay on Criticism,* Part 2, "Be not the first by whom the new is tried; Nor yet the last to lay the old aside." They are not so much concerned with the far-reaching possibilities and uniqueness of the product as with immediate usability issues, such as quality, consistency, and ease of use. Even the later middle majority people are most concerned with the very practical nuts-and-bolts issues, such as delivery schedules, price, and availability. These people are driven by a desire to be *competent.*

The *late adopter* is most concerned with issues of self-protection. She does not want to make a mistake. She is not so concerned with the benefits of the products as she is with not being criticized for her decision. This person wants to *reduce risk.*

The *laggard* will not use a product until virtually forced to do so. He is the kind of person who was told by his clients to "get an e-mail account or I won't do business with you." This person wants *complete safety.*

Let us now look into *the kind of word of mouth that each kind of person needs* to propel him through each step of the decision process.

The Innovator

Deciding to decide. Needs to hear that a product is new, unusual, and that very few other people have heard of it. Needs to hear things like "Did you hear that company X is coming out with a new…?

Weighing information. Usually the innovator is willing to develop the information about the product himself. This is the kind of person who is always trying the latest gadget, for instance. He is often turned on by the following kind of word of mouth: "There's very little known about this, but if you want to get in on the ground floor, here is an opportunity to play with this product."

Trial. This person is turned on by the idea that he will be the first to try the product. "Be the first to try" is a powerful incentive to get involved in the product.

Implementing/ongoing usage. This person is not at all concerned with smooth implementation. He is technological leader and will leave such concerns to "lesser mortals."

Expanding commitment. This person is extremely interested in wild and crazy new uses for the product. He is willing to try almost anything. He can be moved by word of mouth suggesting extremely unusual new uses: "Did you know that X can be used for …."

The Early Adopter

Deciding to decide. Here the initial grabber is the possibility of making a major leap forward in effectiveness. This person wants to hear about the possibilities, appealing to his visionary nature.

Weighing information. The early adopter is quite willing to ignore the fact that the major bugs have not been were worked out. She is willing to accept incomplete documentation. She is willing to be on the initial part of the learning curve with the manufacturer.

Trial. At this point the person is willing to try more for feasibility than for performance.

Implementing/ongoing usage. This person is willing to implement to get the edge over his competition. He is willing to put in his own engineering and other resources that most other customers expect from the manufacturer in order to get the edge over the competition.

Expanding commitment. This type of customer at this stage of the decision process will often roll out very quickly, again to stand out from the rest of the pack.

The Middle Majority

Deciding to decide. This person wants to hear reassurance that the product is ready for "Prime Time."

Weighing information. This type of customer wants to know all about the practicalities of the product.

Trial. This individual is trying not only for product superiority, but for all of the other practicalities such as price, delivery, service, and terms.

Implementing/ongoing usage. This person is very concerned about training and support issues.

Expanding commitment. This individual is not likely to extend the product beyond usual uses until reassured by peers.

The Late Adopter

Deciding to decide. Often, the grabber here is that the person is losing more that he is gaining by not using the product. For example: "The time you will save by getting a laptop will more than make up for the time spent in learning. Now is the time because you are losing a lot now."

Weighing information. This person wants information that it's a mature product or easily serviced.

Trial. The late adopter is often trying to make sure she won't get into trouble, rather than to look for any significant advantages.

Implementing/ongoing usage. This person wants a very low-key implementation. The more invisible, the more successful.

Expanding commitment. This person exhibits a very slow and gradual expansion of use, but very stable once she gets there. She wants to hear that a lot of people are using the product as their standard product in this area.

The Laggard

Deciding to decide. The grabber here is necessity. Everyone is doing it, so he has to do it, or use it.

Weighing information. He is looking for the problems, and reassurance that there are no problems.

Trial. This person won't try anything new. She wants reassurance that everyone else has tried it.

Implementing/ongoing usage. He adopts the product only when he has to.

Expanding commitment. He wants reassurance that he is using it in the standard way.

The Decision Matrix™

If you encourage word-of-mouth messages that tell the innovators that the product is "tried and true," or that tell an early adopter that the product is something that "everyone is using," or that tell a late adopter that the product is "the latest and greatest," you will turn them off. It is important to give the right people the right message at the right point of their decision cycle.

The Decision Matrix™, as shown in Table 5-1, puts the whole decision process together.

Table 5-1
The Decision Matrix™

	Deciding to Decide	Weighing Information	Trial	Implementing	Expanding Commitment
Innovator Wants to be outstanding. Venturesome	Wants to hear how "far out" the product is. *It's so new and unusual, no one's even heard of it or tried it. It works on a totally new principle. Most people wouldn't even under-*	*stand it.*	There is little information to gather. He will have to investigate the product first hand. *It's so far out that there is nothing to compare it to. It's in a different class.*	Wants to be among the first to try. *It is so new that no one has tried it yet. You would be the first.*	Wants to be the pioneer who will lead the way for other people. *Now that you've tried it successfully, you can help others learn about it.*
Early adopter Driven by excellence. Respectful	Concerned more about possibilities than actualities. *Think of the possibilities. If this product really worked in your situation, it would change your life or give you a competitive edge.*	Looking not as much for "hard" information as for a vision of what might be. *Here's how I envision using the product. The other products are more ordinary. This one has*	*possibilities.* Doesn't care that it hasn't been used in his situation, just that it may be applicable. *This product doesn't work all the time. But when it does, wow!*	Like the innovator, also wants to lead the way. Knows there will be problems, wants to know what they are, and how they can be handled. *Here is how to get the most out of it and minimize the problems.*	Wants a major advantage for being at the beginning of the curve. *Here are the additional possibilities that will give you a competitive edge.*
Middle majority Wants to be competent. Deliberate	Concerned with practicalities. *This has been tried and really works in situations like yours, in your industry, etc.*	Wants comparisons about how it's working out in situations similar to his own. *Here is the practical information about how this is working out in the real world.*	Wants to verify that it will work in his situation without investing too much time and trouble. *The bugs have been worked out, and it is highly predictable.*	Wants to know that there is an easy way out if it doesn't work out. *Training, support, and guarantees are in place and reliable.*	Wants to know usage is getting pretty standard. *It is rapidly becoming the standard in our industry*

	Deciding to Decide	Weighing Information	Trial	Implementing	Expanding Commitment
Late majority Wants to reduce risk. Skeptical	Promises a good deal on a tried and true product. *It has become virtually a commodity, and this product can get you better price, delivery, service, training, etc.*	Wants to "shop around" and get the proven product with the best deal. *I've checked out the pricing and service, etc., and it seems to be the best product.*	Tends to be not for product excellence, but centers around the support system. *Check out how wonderful they are to deal with, everyone can fix your problems, etc.*	Wants complete support for rolling out full usage of the product. *They'll come in and do it all for you.*	Wants to use what everyone else is using, in the way that they are using it. *Everybody is using it for everything.*
Laggard Wants to be completely safe. Traditional	Wants reassurance that it is a safe product where nothing will go wrong. *You'll get in trouble if you aren't using this.*	Wants to find the loopholes, problems, negatives, etc. If he doesn't find some, will keep looking. *Here are the risks, and this is how to render them harmless.*	Basically won't try anything new. Needs reassurance that the product is the standard product used in his industry, situation, etc. *Try it, everyone else has and likes it.*	Implements only when he has to. *Adopt this product, or else.*	Wants reassurance that he is using it in the standard way. *That's the way we all use it.*

The idea of the Decision Matrix™ is to get your customers to the next stages of the decision process, using the messages below in the right order, from the right sources. For example, if you are going after early adopters, read across the early adopter row and get people's word of mouth in the order prescribed.

You can use the Decision Matrix™ to zero in on what messages you should be trying to develop and get transmitted. No one, to my knowledge, has ever laid out the stages of the decision cycle against the adopter types to see what messages are needed. I've used it for years as a secret weapon to figure out the messages that will have the most impact in marketing programs. If you use anything at all in this book, I urge you to use this chart. Reproduce it, put it up on your wall (and refer anyone who asks you about it to this book, of course!). If it allows you to sharpen even one message, it could be worth millions of dollars in sales to you. The Decision Matrix™ allows you to zero in on marketing messages of all kinds, particularly in designing word-of-mouth programs.

CHAPTER 6
Delivering the Message

How do you get the word of mouth to people? That question brings us to a consideration of the sources of word of mouth, and then to a consideration of the channels of delivery.

Sources of Word of Mouth

There are three different kinds of word of mouth among customers:

1. Expert to expert

2. Expert to peer

3. Peer to peer

In some situations, experts are the most powerful sources of word of mouth. But in others, local influencers or peers can be even more persuasive. Let's look at the different roles of experts and peers to understand when to use which source.

The Power of Experts

Experts are the most important and leveraged sources of word of mouth. When you have the experts behind you and can get them talking about your product, they will often start a stampede toward your product that is unstoppable.

Every industry has experts who are the prime opinion leaders. It's obvious in professions like medicine, where there are recognized luminaries with whom physicians check before embarking on a new treatment. But even in consumer areas, there are magazine editors, popular trendsetters, and others to whom people look in order to know what's "in" and what's "out."

In order to construct effective word-of-mouth campaigns, you must first understand the function of experts and their unique psychology.

The Expert Is a Different Breed of Cat

The first thing to understand about experts is that they are in the expert business. They want to be experts. It's part of their sense of self. They love being on the cutting edge, having people come to them for the latest word on new developments. Whatever business or profession they are in, they are also in the expert business. In fact, they may spend more time in the expert business than in their regular business or profession.

The expert business is like any other. Experts are continually seeking expert "jobs" (speeches, for example) and are continually seeking to bolster their status as experts, in other words, to market themselves. They spend much of their time giving speeches, seminars, and consulting. They are often prolific writers, which is usually their main marketing method. They are always traveling. Their marketing orientation makes them very approachable, contrary to the common view of them as insulated and difficult to reach.

People think of experts as being formal, pretentious, ivory-tower, inaccessible stuffed shirts. Nothing could be further from the truth. I've worked with hundreds and hundreds of experts, individually and in groups, in dozens of different fields. They are astonishingly easy to reach. Most are informal, friendly, even humorous. They tend to be open about what they know, and surprisingly willing to admit what they don't know. In other words, they tend to be intellectually confident and unthreatened by not knowing something.

They see themselves as visionaries, able to see beyond the horizon to future implications. They are the innovators and very early adopters of new products, ideas, and technologies. As such, they are more than willing to share their experiences and opinions about these new products.

The world . . . is only beginning to see that the wealth of a nation consists more than anything else in the number of geniuses that it harbors . . . . Geniuses are ferments; and when they come together, as they have done in certain lands at certain times, the whole population seems to share in the higher energy which they awaken. The effects are incalculable and often not easy to trace in detail, but they are pervasive and momentous.

—William James

Expert-to-Expert Word of Mouth

He could just as well have been talking about experts. As a psychologist, I have been fascinated by the much-overlooked phenomenon alluded to in the James quote above. I call it the *Experts Critical Mass Effect.* When a group of experts get together, they quickly reach psychological critical mass and create an explosion of new ideas. Some of the more spectacular examples, which have each revolutionized their field at the time and shaken the world, were the Continental Congress, the Manhattan Project, the Bauhaus School, Xerox Parc, the MIT media lab, Disney, Microsoft, Andrew Carnegie's "brain trust," and the Vienna Circle. Experts often tell me that the time they manage to squeeze in at conferences with other experts—in the hallways, lounges, or private dinners—are the most valuable parts of the conferences. The point is that *experts don't get to speak with each other often enough, even though the process is immensely valuable.*

I predict that the importance and value of experts will increase dramatically in the coming years. The increased ability to generate and access information brought about by computer and telecommunication advances has generated an information overload. As this information overload increases, experts will become even more important, because experts can filter, distill, and synthesize vast amounts of data. Data has to be turned into information, which has to be turned into knowledge, which has to be turned into wisdom. Unfortunately, at this point of human development, wisdom is lagging far behind data. Experts are our main catalysts for converting data into wisdom. As information increases, interactive groups of experts become increasingly necessary to cover each area. But experts groups are difficult to convene, since experts are so busy.

Fortunately, hidden in the cause of the information overload problem is its solution. If the causes of the problem are computers and telecommunication, the very technology that created the problem can be used to solve it. This is the first time in human history that experts can easily be brought together: The audio teleconferences finally reached a high level of quality and convenience. So have computer conferences, and soon video teleconferences will be as easy as regular conference calls.

Change the opinion of a relatively small handful of experts, and you'll change the entire marketplace.

What does this mean for word of mouth and your product? Experts are a focused, leveraged source of influence. Change the opinion of a relatively small handful of experts, and you'll change the entire marketplace.

I'm convinced that convenient forums of experts need to be developed to predict—and even accelerate—innovation. Experts are very busy, yet the demand for their services will increase. However, a tremendous amount of their time is wasted on travel.

A clearinghouse is needed to bring experts together, harness their power, allow them to synergize and potentiate each other, and to reduce redundancy (answering the same questions over and over).

In the not too distant future, experts will be able to read a printout of the daily remarks of colleagues on a screen, then dictate their responses into their notebook computers, wherever they are in the world. They'll be able to set up a conference call whenever they want in order to brainstorm or discuss issues more interactively. Interested companies will sponsor some of the sessions, while other sessions will be private, for the benefit of the experts only.

The point here is that you have an unprecedented opportunity to "capture" these increasingly important people and have them work to your advantage.

How to "Capture" the Experts in Your Field

You have a tremendous opportunity for starting what I have been calling since 1986 an "Xperts Xchange" (no relation to the Experts Exchange on the Internet, which is a great idea) in your field of endeavor. It is an opportunity for you to get the experts on your team and have them participate in the development and launch of new products.

You can fund the exchange of new ideas in your field. Organize and fund the forum (audio teleconference, computer conference, etc.) that gets the experts together. It can be surprisingly inexpensive for the payoff involved.

You can get a preview of the cutting-edge thinking in your field, hear what the experts are recommending, and even influence their recommendations.

There are many ways to do this. For instance, you can hold a regular teleconference of the experts in a given field, which you then make available to the rest of the industry. I have conducted many experts' sessions that I then sold to the entire industry. Another approach is to bring them together into a private advisory group.

Expert-to-Peer and Peer-to-Peer Word of Mouth

There is a two-step process in experience gathering via word of mouth. First people want to know what the upside potential of the product is. They speak of this as its "promise." Here, they look toward the company to make the claim, or promise, and the expert to confirm this upside potential. But that is not enough for a decision because the endorsement of the expert only says to the decision maker that under ideal conditions, in an expert's hands, the claims are true. Next, the decision maker still has to decide whether the promise will be fulfilled in the real world—the more typical world—of his experience. He also wants to know where the pitfalls are. This process can only be achieved by hearing peers on one's own level, or by direct experience. It usually takes years to go from initial interest to trial to adoption, because it takes an inordinate amount of time to talk with so many people, and to gather their experiences.

Table 6-1 shows the sources of word of mouth, their functions, and the content.

Table 6-1 Sources of Word of Mouth.		
Source	**Function**	**Content (what it provides)**
Company advocates	Information	The claims, the benefits
Experts	Confirmation	The upside and downside potential under the *best circumstances.*
Peers	Verification	What to expect in the *real world*, in typical situations.

Delivery of Word of Mouth

The following flow of the most persuasive combination in marketing can compress a many-year process into a few weeks or months:

- Initial information from an expert

- Followed by organized trial

- Followed by a means of pooling peer experience (to multiply it, put it into context, and give practical tips and suggestions)

That flow is the way to accelerate the experience gathering and evaluation that people need in order to adopt your product. But this flow rarely happens naturally. If it does, it often takes many, many years.

How to Deliver This Potent Combination

It is possible to accelerate "natural" word of mouth by creating events and materials that stimulate, amplify, and deliver word of mouth, thereby accelerating it. This formula—experts' endorsement, trial, and peer experience pooling—can be delivered in many ways, such as audio teleconferences, printed roundtables, Web sites, and many other means.

This kind of approach, in contrast to the promotional "sit them down and make them listen to a sales pitch" approach, only works with products that can benefit from objective scrutiny. But when it does work, it is the most spectacular, honest, responsible, and lasting means of increasing sales you ever saw! With the right type of product, you may be able to cut your advertising, sales time, and all other promotion to the bare minimum, or cut them out entirely. This powerful method will be explained in more detail in Chapter 9.

Champions

Champions are customers, influencers, recommenders, or prescribers who are actively trying to get other people to buy and use your product. They are the prime movers of your word of mouth.

Earlier in this book, I raised the rhetorical question, "If you consider word of mouth to be the most powerful force in the marketplace, how come you don't have a Vice President of Word of Mouth?" Here, I'd like to suggest that after you put in a Vice President of Word of Mouth, you also install a Director of Champions. You should be aggressively identifying and tracking your champions. While most companies have a procedure for logging complaint letters, there is usually no procedure for logging letters of praise. These letters, as well as all similar communications to your company, should be logged, acknowledged, and special steps should be taken to give the authors of these letters special treatment. I know some companies that invite their champions to a hotel buffet, and that have a video crew waiting to tape individual testimonials, with permission, of course.

Identify these people through marketing research, sales research, and any other means you can. Don't stop short by just finding out that "a friend" recommended your service to a new customer. Find out, specifically, what friend and reward that person as well. When you find several people who are getting other people to become your customers, contact those people. Interview them either individually or in focus groups and find out exactly what they have said. After all, they have actually sold your product to other people! It's very useful if you can interview, together in a group, both the champions and the people to whom the recommendations were made. That way, you can hear what people actually said and hear what was going through the minds of the new customers, particularly what "grabbed" them.

You should be in continual contact with these people. Get specific testimonials from them that are needed to overcome identified blocks in your prospects' decision process. Get them to serve on advisory boards. Get them to serve as references. Let them beta test your products. Give them preferential treatment in any way you can. Hire them, when you can.

Why Traditional Media Lose Effectiveness

Many products are at a point where they just won't respond cost-effectively to conventional marketing methods. This can happen anywhere from before the product launch to years into the product life cycle.

With some products, it becomes evident before launch that the product, its message, or the steps necessary to persuade the customer are too complex for your salespeople, ads, or other conventional selling media to be effective.

Even after a product has been out for a while, you can keep pouring more and more money into conventional media, without much visible result. You can change your ad campaign, media mix, sales message, sales aids, and brochures. You may even try alternative approaches, such as experts' endorsements, symposia, sampling, free trials, or demonstrations. You keep thinking you haven't found the right message, or the right way to present it. Often at this point, people mistakenly think they have a "positioning" problem.

You probably have *awareness* and *interest,* but little *trial* and *adoption.* The only thing that people are adopting is a "wait and see" attitude.

In this day and age, the problem rarely is getting the *information* about the benefits of your product across to your potential customers. That's easy. It just takes money for enough salespeople, ads, mailings, or PR. But you quickly reach diminishing returns, where throwing more money at potential customers produces little result.

Creating interest in your product isn't so hard either: All it takes is the promise of something different about your product that might actually make a difference to your customer.

Serious *trial, evaluation, adoption,* and *expansion* of use are other matters entirely. These latter stages of decision making are hellishly difficult to move people through. Conventional marketing methods are relatively ineffective during these stages. *This is where most products are stuck.*

Why are conventional methods relatively ineffective in the latter stages of adoption? Because conventional marketing methods are mostly directed at getting across *information*: the features, claims, and benefits of your product. But *information is not enough.* The information must:

- Come from the right source

- Be presented in the right sequence

- Be relevant to the particular customer

- Be credible

- Be presented in a context in which the customer is receptive

Confirmation and Verification

Often even the right information presented in the right way is still not enough. Past a certain point, you begin to spin your wheels. Why?

Once people have heard of your product and its claims (information), they need confirmation and verification: *confirmation* from independent sources that the claims are valid, and *verification* that the product will do the job it promises to do in their particular situation. These are the two major phases of the product adoption cycle, and you are probably only covering the first phase:

1. The *Information Phase* (awareness and interest) is the learning phase in which information is gathered. This is where the customer considers whether he is interested in the product, what benefits it may have to him, whether it is worth finding out more. The major mental set is: "If the claims are true, would I want it?" This is the phase that marketers

address most of the time, to the almost total neglect of the
second phase.

2. The *Verification Phase* (trial, evaluation, and adoption) is
the second phase, where the customer is trying to find out
if the claims are true. The conventional kind of information that marketers try to provide is almost totally irrelevant to this phase.

Why?

■ Prospects already have most of the information. They need
verification, which they think they can't get from you,
because you are not objective.

■ They need verification from an independent source. In their
attempts to verify the truth, information must be perceived
to be objective in order to be believed.

■ Most marketing is advocacy.

■ Advocacy is not perceived to be objective.

■ Therefore, most marketing is not viewed as objective.

■ Therefore, most marketing is not believed.

What Is Objectivity?

Objectivity is accurate, complete, and clear presentation of the
relevant facts and conclusions, in other words, an unbiased evaluation of the advantages, disadvantages, and value of the products.

It's not that people don't believe that what you are saying is
true. In some industries, such as the pharmaceutical industry,
there are severe penalties for giving inaccurate information and
for lies of omission. But, there are many ways to slant the truth
and put a spin on things. And even though it can happen unin-
tentionally and from the noble motives of enthusiasm for your

product and a desire for people to reap its benefits, most people would no more take at face value a manufacturer's evaluation of his own product than they would leave a fox to watch the chicken coop.

There are several ways that people try to get the objective information they need. They are:

1. Direct experience with the product

2. Experience of peers who are like themselves

3. Experts' experience

4. Scientific journals, studies, panels

5. Independent rating and opinion services

So, the necessary objectivity is provided only by something that delivers independent experience and evaluation.

Let's recap:

- You need to get your prospects beyond information gathering

- To confirmation and verification

- Which customers get by objective, independent experience and evaluation

- Which conventional marketing does not deliver

Therefore, what keeps most superior products with stagnant sales from reaching full market share is not the time it takes people to find out about your product. It is the inordinate amount of time it takes the decision makers to get the *independent experience* to confirm and verify the truth of what you are saying.

People are caught in a dilemma. A physician, for instance, will not get experience with a drug unless she has confidence in it, but she can't get confidence in it unless she has experience with it.

If what holds products back is the time it takes to get experience, the problem becomes how to accelerate that experience gathering.

How to Accelerate Experience Gathering

Some points in the next two sections received mention above but deserve some reiteration here. Basically, there are only two ways for your customers to get experience: directly or indirectly (vicariously).

Direct Experience

The two traditional ways of accelerating the accumulation of direct experience are *demonstrations* and *free trial*. These methods can be extremely effective, as every marketer knows. They are powerful because they provide experience, which can conclusively provide the verification and confirmation that people need to make a decision. But demos and trial also have several disadvantages. Demonstrations are not always possible. For instance, there may not be anything to see in a demo, as in the case of some drugs. Even when the product can be demonstrated, the demo is often inconclusive. Conditions are often artificial, as at trade shows and dealers, where the demonstrator may have more skill than the customer—which means that the decision maker does not know whether the product will work the same way in the real world. From the point of view of the marketer, there is little control over the demonstrator, who may be a dealer or a rep who is not as skilled or motivated as you would like.

Free trial (sampling, equipment loans, etc.), as powerful as it can be, also has its own set of difficulties. There are many things that are impossible or difficult to try or sample, such as life insurance, a new surgical procedure, or any other all-or-nothing major commitments. Often, products that one would think are easy to try, such as new prescription drugs, involve a large perceived risk, which makes people like physicians and pharmacists want to wait, even when you give samples. Also, as many consumer packaged-goods marketers have learned, samples and coupons are often used by people who are already customers, thereby cutting into regular sales without stimulating new triers.

Often, demos and trials tend to make the customer want to try other products as well, increasing the time it takes for a commitment.

Indirect Experience

In an effort to reduce the risks inherent in direct experience gathering (such as directly trying the product), and also in an effort to broaden the experience to a wider sample, customers and prospects often go to indirect experience gathering. They will seek the opinions of experts, ask their peers, and consult independent rating services. They will use the various forms of word of mouth.

Most marketers agree that word of mouth is the most powerful force in the marketplace. The conventional explanation is that it is more credible. That's true as far as it goes. But remember, word of mouth indirectly supplies the independent experience necessary for confirmation and verification, which in turn is necessary for opinion change, which is necessary for behavior change (action, purchase, etc.).

To summarize, the flow goes like this:

Information →

Confirmation/verification of your claims/promises →

Indirect trial (word of mouth) and direct trial →

Belief/opinion change (persuasion) →

Action/behavior (motivation) →

The problem with most indirect experience gathering is that it is out of your control. In fact, that's precisely why word of mouth is so valued by the decision maker. Word of mouth is independent of the seller, and so it's more objective. This is where prospects feel that they can get the real story. Unless you know how to handle it, as soon as you try to control it, it loses its independence and its credibility.

Like a forest fire, word of mouth is smoldering, burning, or blazing along on its own, the most powerful force in the marketplace, out of your control. You never know when it might strike, or what potential good it might do, whether it's even there, what form it's taking, or whether it's actually helping or hurting. But word of mouth can be harnessed.

Above All, You Need a "Story"

Getting across the right message to the right people in the correct adoption cycle, from the right sources, and in the right sequence, can be an impossibly complicated task. Left to their own devices, most word-of-mouth chain reactions never reach the critical mass they need to get started. They just fizzle.

There is a device, however, that allows you to take everything and tie it up into a neat package. That device is called the "Story."

Every medium has a summary device that allows the message to be transmitted and gets the message into the mind of the customer. Good advertising picks the most important benefit of the product and dramatizes it. A good salesperson marshals a compelling argument to persuade a prospect to buy the product. PR emphasizes a newsworthy aspect of the product situation.

Similarly, every word-of-mouth program needs a "story." The story has to have certain characteristics. It has to be:

- *Short and simple*, in order to survive transmission from one person to another without distortion.

- *Interesting, exciting, new, different, unique, or otherwise worth talking about.* If you want people talking about your product, you want to give them something to talk about.

- *In story form.* This is not absolutely necessary, but stories transmit better person-to-person than anything else. People like telling stories, and people like listening to stories. There is something tremendously compelling about a story. When people are listening to an abstract product description, their critical faculties are in high gear. But when they are listening to a story, there is a much lower level of vigilance and critical thinking. They relax. After all, it's just a story. The focus is not on critiquing. The only thing to be judged is whether it's interesting and whether it's true. Truth, however, is not much of an issue when the story is being told by a trusted source. Besides, some stories are so interesting that it doesn't matter much if they are true. In literature, it's called fiction.

However in marketing, ultimately, the story *must be true.* There is no place for fiction in word of mouth marketing. "The truth will out."

Just about everyone in marketing has heard the story about the woman who returned a tire to Nordstrom's. Her money was cheerfully refunded. This would not be unusual, except for the fact that Nordstrom's does not sell tires!

There are similar stories about Rolls Royce, Federal Express, and many other companies.

The story does not have to take the form of an anecdote. It might be an explanation of how a new device works, or a fantasy about the possible uses of a new product for the innovators, or a description of an experiment that proves something about the effectiveness or safety of the product to the middle majority. Or it could be tips, tricks, or suggestions. It can be anything that people will find interesting enough to want to tell each other.

A major part of the creative process in designing word-of-mouth programs and campaigns is to uncover the kinds of stories that will prove compelling to the different types of adopters in their various stages of the decision process. In that vein, let me tell a story to illustrate my point. (Didn't you relax when you read that I am going to tell you a story?)

A CASE IN POINT

I was designing a series of word-of-mouth sessions (this technique will be described in Chapter 9) for a pharmaceutical client. The client had a Parkinson's disease medication, which it manufactured in both tablet and capsule form. Because it had a patent on the manufacture of the tablets, all other competitors could manufacture the drug only in capsule form. The company told me that there was absolutely no advantage to the tablets over the capsules. They just manufactured both because some people prefer one or the other, and it simply gave physicians greater choice.

As part of an audio teleconference group discussion with the world's leading experts on the disease, I asked the experts whether they used tablets or capsules. It turned out that they all used tablets. They pointed out that, unlike capsules, tablets could be broken in half. They proceeded to provide tips on how to use tablets to adjust the dosage of the drug, how they keep track of adjustments using half tablets as their unit of measurement, and similar useful suggestions.

Here the "story" is a series of useful tricks that will make life easier for both the patient and doctor. We played a tape-recorded excerpt of this part of the experts' conversation in hundreds of word-of-mouth small-group teleconferences of physicians. Sales of the clients' tablets went up sixfold, and all of the competitors' sales went down. Two competitors dropped out of the market. And, yes, all of the clients' sales increases were of the tablets, not the capsules.

You might think that uncovering this story was an unusually fortuitous happening. On the contrary, with good products there are invariably such stories, which illustrate product advantages and compel people to use the product. These types of stories are what you want to get people telling each other.

The Science of Memes

There is a whole science that looks at the kinds of ideas that replicate rapidly through a society, primarily via word of mouth. It's called the science of "memes." Memes are ideas that create the conditions that tend to cause their own replication. They are important to any serious consideration of word of mouth.

The first book to describe the concept of the meme is by Richard Dawkins, called *The Selfish Gene.* A very interesting and readable description is also contained in Richard Brodie's *Virus of the Mind.*

For instance, what if there is a crisis that affects us all, but that requires a concerted effort of all of us to counteract the threat? It is not only important for each of us to get the idea that there is such a crisis, but it becomes equally important to "spread the word" —to convince others of the reality of the crisis—in order to get the maximum number of people involved, in order to lessen the threat.

What about a product whose value increases according to how many people have it? Now keep in mind that most things increase in value due to rarity. Some things, however, are not valuable until many, if not most, people have them, as is true, for example, of the fax machine, a particular computer operating system, e-mail, or a word processing format. If you can enlist people to spread the word because it will make your product more valuable to them, you have a powerful formula for selling your product. So, if you can make the argument that if everyone adopts your product it will be easier to interchange parts, to repair, and to borrow available replacements from other people, you have a powerful argument for the adoption of your product.

Brodie mentions five situations in which the spreading of ideas is important to our survival. These are (Brodie's situations, but my descriptions):

- *Crisis*—the quick reaction needed by many people requires the spreading of the idea that the crisis is imminent.

- *Mission*—the concerted effort of many people needed to accomplish major goals requires that the idea of the mission be rapidly spread and accepted by as many people as possible.

- *Problem*—those situations in which the rapid involvement of many people is desirable. It is also extremely gratifying to communicate the solution of widespread problems to large numbers of other people who might have similar problems.

- *Danger*—similarly, the knowing about potential dangers can significantly increase the safety of each person when large numbers of people know about it. Also, people like to protect other people. So the idea of danger tends to get rapidly communicated.

- *Opportunity*—many opportunities increase in value when other people know about them. Many do not. For instance, when you know that a particular company is likely to be successful, you might recommend its stock to large numbers of people *after* you have bought the stock yourself. Before that, you might keep it a secret, the opposite of a meme.

So, consider the following two statements. Which one is likely to be spread?

1. Word of mouth is the most powerful force in the marketplace. It is instructive to study word of mouth because the subject is fascinating. Someday, it will be a major branch of marketing, studied in every business school in the country. Right now, almost no one approaches word of

mouth in an organized manner, so you can use it as a secret weapon.

2. Word of mouth is the most powerful force in the marketplace, much more powerful than salespeople, advertising, and all other marketing elements put together. Your product will live or die because of word of mouth. It is therefore imperative that you expose every significant person in your company—and other colleagues in whose success you would like to have a hand—to the ideas in this book, so that creating word of mouth can become the primary marketing mission. Not only will the acceptance of the ideas in this book be able to save your company enormous amounts of wasted marketing dollars, while making your marketing more effective, the ideas in this book will annihilate your company if your competitors implement the ideas in this book *before you do.*

Obviously, the second statement incorporates all five of the above motivations for spreading the idea of encouraging people to read this book. The lesson here is to not only spread ideas through word of mouth, but also build into those ideas reasons for people to convince others of the value of not only accepting the idea but of also passing it along and convincing others.

Do not only spread ideas through word of mouth, but also build into the idea reasons for people to convince others of the value of not only accepting the idea but of also passing it along and convincing others.

This process, in a word, is called *evangelism.* It doesn't apply only to religions. If you don't turn people into evangelists and motivate them to proselytize, your product has almost no hope, unless your competitors do worse.

Other Kinds of Ideas That Tend to Have "Legs"

Try to build into the ideas that you are trying to spread these sub-categories of the above five situations:

News

Unique results, effects, or activities

Sex

Secrets

Helping others

The unusual

CHAPTER 7

Viral Marketing

If marketing is warfare—and I truly hate that analogy, but it fits in this specific context—then word of mouth is biological warfare. There are ideas that spread so fast, there is almost no stopping them. They cross borders and become worldwide so fast that it almost seems that everyone is talking about the idea at once. In fact, many people are beginning to refer to certain types of marketing as "viral marketing." What kind of ideas are "contagious" and how can they be spread?

First of all, let's look at the scope of what is possible.

There are certain products, primarily Internet services at this point, that have spread to tens of millions of people around the world in a matter of weeks! Netscape Navigator, the e-mail service Hotmail, and many other programs and services have been spread in a way that is being increasingly called "viral marketing." What this means is that in the very act of using the product, there are certain built-in components that cause people to either recommend the product to others or imply a certain recommendation. For instance, whenever someone sends an e-mail through Hotmail, a free Internet e-mail service, at the bottom of the screen there is a phrase that says "Get Free E-mail and Do More on The Web. Visit http://www.msn.com." That's basically all there is to it. That, coupled with an extraordinarily simple Web site and an easy way of enrolling, are the ingredients of something that can spread faster than a plague.

Why? In the very act of using the service, you are sending a message to—infecting, if you will—interested parties who might want free e-mail to sign up.

Another example is RealPlayer™. There are many Web sites that offer audio clips. Most of these are offered in the RealPlayer format. If you don't have it, most Web sites allow you to download it immediately for free. Contained in the free version are opportunities for you to get an upgrade to a fancier version for a nominal fee. Another example is Adobe Acrobat®. It is so ubiquitous that people who would like to post formatted documents to the Web are virtually forced to buy the version that formats into Adobe Acrobat (.pdf) format.

There are numerous other products that fit the viral marketing model, such as many kids' fads. It has been true of the yo-yo for many decades. In fact, yo-yos had a gigantic and rapid resurgence when the ball-bearing axle was invented, making them sleep much longer and thereby enabling tricks to be performed much more easily. The popularity of yo-yos is almost entirely driven by word of mouth.

It's very instructive to look at the principles behind this kind of idea spread, even if viral marketing does not directly apply to your product. There are certain things you may be able to build into your marketing, even if it can't fit exactly the pattern of viral marketing.

How to Spread Ideas Like the Plague

What kinds of ideas, products and conditions cause this kind of idea replication?

- ■ The idea must be something intriguing, compelling, what someone would want to try, or something that is in some other way self-evidently desirable.

- It must be extremely easy to try.

- It must be possible to try it immediately.

- It must be possible to try it without risk.

- Just like the spread of any infectious disease, people have to be in close contact, though not necessarily physically. Just as yo-yos spread easily through the schoolyard because kids are in physical proximity, ideas can spread over the Internet because people are now in close communication proximity. Similarly, ideas can spread fast in a national convention because all of the movers and shakers are right there.

- The very use of the product exposes *new* people to not only its desirability but also its *trial mechanism*.

What is the implication for your product?

- Find a compelling idea.

- Make it easy for people to try—or otherwise experience—your product immediately and without friction or risk.

- Spread this idea where people are in close contact, or at least close communication, taking advantage of existing communication channels.

- Make the very act of using the product a way of creating new triers.

Viral Marketing on the Internet

1. Adam Frankl invented a game called Roger Wilco, which is a fighter pilot game that can be played across the

Internet with others around the world. Users can link up into conference calls so that they can hear each other's reactions.

He posted a copy of his program on a freeware Web site on May 3, 1999. He invited people to try it free, and then to forward it to as many friends as possible so that they could all play together. This triggered a speed-of-light chain reaction: In 24 hours the program was downloaded by 2,800 people in forty-six countries from www.roger wilco.com. In 30 days it had spread to 100,000 people. At that rate, it could spread to millions in a matter of months. Presumably, a substantial fraction of these people can be converted to paying customers eventually.

2. Geocities (bought by Yahoo! for $4 billion in stock) has home pages for more than 4 million users.

3. The eBay auction site requires *both* buyers and sellers. If you are a seller, it's in your interest to get as many people interested as possible. One of the reasons that people tell others about eBay is that they want to have the maximum number of people participating.

4. Instant messaging software is a perfect example of viral marketing, since your friends or colleagues have to be on the same software. Examples are AOL instant messenger, ICQ (reportedly used by more than 35 million people, bought by AOL for $400 million), and Microsoft's MSN Messenger Service.

5. Hotmail, bought by Microsoft for $400 Million is, as of this writing, reportedly serving 75 million people and signing up more than a hundred thousand people a day!

6. Napster, a way of networking people's hard drives so that they can share music, has spread so fast in only a few

months that it has threatened the entire recording industry and appeared on the cover of Newsweek!

7. Winamp makes it easier to download digitized music if your friends use it too.

8. Six Degrees has grown to millions of users, all by getting people to bring their friends and business associates into circles for discussions.

9. Third Voice gives away a program that lets people attach the equivalent of stick-on notes to Web pages, so that other users of the program can see them. This lets people attach comments, criticism, wisecracks, and other messages to other people's Web sites, much to the consternation of the owners of the Web sites. But you have to have the software to read the comments.

10. Gizmoz, from something called the ViralCasting Network, gives little animated mini-presentations that people can paste onto their Web sites, e-mail to friends, put on greeting cards, etc. They are catching on like wildfire, but they're difficult to describe. Look at them at www.gizmoz.com.

11. There are multiple free fax services that attach an ad to the bottom of the fax. Some of the services are ifaxmail.com, efax.com, and jfax.com.

12. Almost every article and download, and many other sites on the Internet, have (or should have) a "share this with a friend" button.

13. There are numerous e-greeting card companies springing up. Every time someone gets one, he is likely to get "hooked" and send one on to someone else, with just a click of a link.

These sites are spreading so fast, and mutating like viruses, that by the time you read this book there are bound to be many more examples and many more approaches invented. So, I've set up a special page on our Web site so that you can stay current on viral marketing. It's www.mnav.com/viralmarketing.htm. Send it to a friend!

Word of Mouth on the Internet

It's almost as if the Internet was invented for word of mouth. And it was. Originally, it was a worldwide network of scientists "talking" among themselves to share scientific information. It was invented to accelerate communication, but communication was slow at first. It wasn't until it was opened up to the rest of us for commercial communication and the World Wide Web was invented that the Internet took off. At that point, its growth was so explosive that it broke all records for the adoption of innovations. Most of the growth was through word of mouth. After all, no one owns it, so no one advertised it.

Several commercial products that made use of the Internet became bestsellers, most of them having been offered for free at first. The Internet was both the means of transmitting the news about the product and its ordering and delivery mechanism. So, for instance, Eudora became the dominant e-mail manager and Mosaic, then Netscape Navigator, then Internet Explorer, became the dominant Web browsers. Yahoo!, Lycos, and Altavista became the dominant directory and search engines, supplanted almost overnight by Google, again by word of mouth.

E-mail proliferated, Web sites multiplied, and chat rooms, list groups, and other discussion sites mushroomed.

Then some very interesting things started to happen. The Internet made individual and group communication so much easier that word of mouth began to get built into various features of the Internet. For instance, many Web sites now include features that could be called, in Nicholas Negreponte's words, "electronic word of mouth." Many sites feature collaborative filtering (also known as group filtering). This means that hundreds of thousands of people, eventually millions, all rate movies, books, music, and other things that involve a high degree of personal taste and subjectivity. You go on the Web site and rate a large number of movies, for instance. Then, you can request the rating of movies that you haven't seen yet. The program on the Web site looks into its database and finds the few people who have the ratings most similar to your past ratings and who have seen movies that you have not rated. It presents you with a list of the movies that they have rated highest that you have not rated. Some of these, of course, you will have seen. So you simply rate them, further refining your profile. However, others you will not have seen. There is a very high probability that you will like the movies that these people have liked because they have liked the movies that you have liked and hated the ones that you have hated. They have, in effect, recommended the movie to you. It is astounding how well this kind of thing works. I predict that this will be a major force in the Internet, applied to all sorts of areas once people understand its power and figure out how to describe it.

Other Web sites build word of mouth into their design. There are, for instance, increasing numbers of expert Web sites. Here, with a variety of schemes, people are able to tap into the expertise of large numbers of people. Sometimes, people earn credits for giving useful answers, which they can then use to get their own questions answered. There is no question that this usage will increase radically, making many people who understand the phenomenon of word of mouth incredibly rich in the process.

The Web is the perfect medium for viral marketing. If you have a product that can be distributed on the Web, where the very act of using the product is a demo that can include a pitch to sign up for or buy the product, you have a perfect recipe for runaway word of mouth.

The eBay auction site also has a very interesting built-in word-of-mouth technique. The success of the site depends upon a high degree of trust on the part of both the buyer and seller. Thus, it has buyers rate sellers and sellers rate buyers. First-time participants are flagged as such, and the buyers or sellers know that they are assuming a higher degree of risk. Buyers rate sellers on such things as the accuracy of their descriptions, their courtesy, or the promptness of their delivery. Sellers rate buyers on the promptness of their payments and how easy they were to do business with. You will see an increase in this kind of word of mouth on the Internet.

There are also countless Usenet groups discussing thousands of different subjects. This is another place for the word to spread, both positively and negatively. You better have people monitoring the ones that are relevant to you, or things can get quickly out of hand. Here's an example of both at the same time. I once had a problem with delivery of a Dell laptop. I got on the Dell Usenet group and mentioned that I was getting several conflicting stories about the delay. I recommended that people not buy that particular laptop. A Dell vice president called back within hours. She apologized, offered the use of a loaner, and resolved the problem to more than my satisfaction. I have standardized on Dell computers for our office and have bought many more since. The point here is that all forums are places where negative word of mouth can run rampant or be turned around to great advantage.

E-mail has taken word of mouth to another level also, as illustrated by the following.

A CASE IN POINT

Since I happen to be the workshop chairman of the Society of American Magicians in New York, let me tell you how it works with magicians. As you can imagine, magicians are a very secretive bunch of people, but as secretive as they are with nonmagicians, they are extremely giving with each other. When I want to notify my fellow magicians around New York of something new and interesting that I have heard of, I have a distribution list set up in my e-mail program. To send to the few hundred people is literally no more difficult then sending to one person. If I want to tell magicians all over the world about something, I can send e-mail to a secret worldwide listgroup of more than 7000 magicians. Again, it is no more difficult than sending to one friend. As a result, "the word" about new books, videotapes, television programs, and techniques spreads to knowledgeable magicians almost immediately. As an example, the identity of the Masked Magician was correctly identified within a few hours of his appearance on television. People recognized his mannerisms, others recognized equipment they had sold him, and so on. Also, whenever someone identifies a source of equipment used by magicians on the Web, he publishes the URL and sends the others e-mails containing the URL.

Word of mouth has truly reached instantaneous and global proportions.

If you don't think that word of mouth in the Internet is here to stay, take a look at www.deja.com and www.epinions.com. They are truly institutionalized word of mouth. On deja.com, you can look up ratings on almost anything that you want to buy, and read comments of real people. I found it to be extraordinarily accurate in describing the differences between the car that I got rid of and the car that I bought, and will be using it for future purchases.

Six Things You Should Be Doing to Benefit from Word of Mouth on the Internet

1. Assign people to monitor every forum, listgroup, and other Internet discussion medium that could possibly influence your product sales. Some will be restricted to customers only, so that you can't get into them. In that

case try to get one of your customers to at least report to you or send you copies of relevant information.

2. Build in various word-of-mouth attributes into your Web site. Doing this will not only make your Web site more valuable, it will give it extra credibility.

3. Sprinkle testimonials and endorsements all over your Web site. However, consonant with the teaching in the rest of this book, approach it systematically. Make sure that the messages fit the stage of the decision cycle and the adoption category of the customers you are trying to convince.

4. If you don't know how to do it already, drop everything and learn how to set up distribution lists in your e-mail program. Set up lists of business associates, friends, and various categories of customers. Send out regular short notes informing people of things that are genuinely useful. Ask people to pass along the word to *their* distribution lists. If you have a long message, post it on your Web site and e-mail people the address of that page.

5. Use your Web site to get across and demonstrate all of the extraordinary things that you are doing that will get people talking. Remember, people only go out of their way to talk about the UNusual, EXTRAordinary, and OUTrageous.

6. Plug into experts and services that recommend products to their constituencies. Learn about infomediaries and plug into them.

Non-Internet Viral Marketing

Do you think viral marketing is relevant only to the Internet? How about the Palm Pilot™ (now the Palm)? If you own the

Palm, you want everyone to have one, so that they can beam their business card to you, or so you can get software you want to try out beamed to you. People meet each other, teach each other how to beam, and share programs. I was in a meeting at a major corporation recently, and they asked for my business card. I asked if they had Palm Pilots. Fifteen people pulled them out, and I beamed my electronic business card, which has more information than is on my regular business card, to all of them. Palm users actively try to get people to adopt the Palm so that everyone can have the same standard.

I have now given up my Palm in favor of a Pocket PC™. It cleverly has a program called Peacekeeper that allows people to beam across Palm and Pocket PC platforms. It's much better integrated into the windows environment, has much better memory, and has such a good display that I have already read a novel on it! When people see it, they instantly want one. It's in my interest to spread the word because if it is successful it will be the e-book standard, and there will be many more programs developed for it. If it is handled right, it will be a tremendous success because it is so much better than the Palm technology, while actually being simpler to use for Windows users.

With any product where people can benefit from everybody having the same standard, you can sometimes activate word of mouth by making the argument that people need to get other people on the same standard so that it all works. Thus, the product message has a built-in motivator for replication and contagion, as well as a built-in mechanism for excluding your competitors!

CHAPTER 8

Researching Word of Mouth

What Do People Talk About?

People talk about the extraordinary, surprising, astonishing, amazing, unusual, bizarre, remarkable, wonderful, and incredible. These are the things they have the most energy around. They do not tend to talk about the ordinary. The ordinary is BOOOORRING! This means that if your service is satisfactory, people won't talk about it. It has to be unusually poor or unusually good for it to be "worth talking about."

Therefore, you have to train your people, and give them the right incentives, to go out of their way to do things that are so constructively outrageous that people will talk about them. For instance, you might want to have a weekly or monthly reward for the most outrageous positive thing that one of your employees does for a customer.

Space does not permit a long list of customer service tips. There are many wonderful books on customer service, filled with tips on things that you can do to create great, even outrageous, service. I recommend *Positively Outrageous Service*, by T. Scott Gross.

Great customer service is not a policy or set of rules. It is an attitude. It is spread from the top of the company down in a series of actions by the top people in the company, as well as by singling out, communicating, and rewarding acts of extraordinary service. If your company does not have its own Nordstrom's and FedEx stories, *you need to take immediate steps to make sure that such incidents take place, and that they are identified, communicated, and rewarded.*

The stories alluded to above, which were briefly mentioned earlier, bear repeating. An elderly lady returned an automobile tire to Nordstrom's. Since she did not have any sales receipts, the clerk simply asked for how much she had paid. She told him, and, taking her word for it, he cheerfully refunded her money. Nothing extraordinary so far, except that most stores would not have even gone this far. What is really extraordinary is that Nordstrom's does not carry automobile tires! This story was popularized by Tom Peters and was worth several million dollars in free publicity; the tire cost Nordstrom's about twenty-nine dollars. In fact, it was the first time that many Easterners like me had ever heard of Nordstrom's. What do you think my attitude was when a Nordstrom's opened 15 minutes from my house?

The FedEx story is about a package that was discovered left on the airport tarmac after a FedEx plane had departed from Alaska. An employee took out his credit card, rented a helicopter and delivered the package personally. Again, millions of dollars of publicity from a $2,000 investment.

We were once running a salesperson teleconference for Roche Laboratories. One key salesperson could not be contacted. Through a persistent series of phone calls, we finally tracked him down to a coffee shop in Hawaii. We simply put him in the conference without comment. Later, after a series of promotions, he became a major client and recommended our services to many of his colleagues.

And here is my favorite "Nordstrom's story": Homegrocer.com, the Internet grocery shopping service based in Seattle (now owned by WebVan), was supplying food for a party run by one of their customers. They received an urgent call that the centerpiece of the entire party, a gigantic smoked salmon, was missing from the order. They immediately discovered that the salmon had been left behind. Terry Drayton, their president, put the salmon in his car and delivered it personally. When he got there, he discovered that the customer was Mrs. Nordstrom!

Negative Word of Mouth

Just as you should put special attention on creating identifying and communicating positive stories that illustrate your company's greatest strengths, you should have a special system to identify actual and potential negative word of mouth.

Retailers retain "mystery shoppers" who shop at their stores and report on the experience. Similarly, you should retain a service to check on how your phone calls and other interactions are handled. I just signed up for a new Internet service provider and Web host. I had to call their technical support several times and was handled extraordinarily well. When I next checked my e-mail, there was a short questionnaire for each of the technical service calls, asking not only about the specific service, but also about the person who answered my call. I'm sure that they can identify bad apples almost instantly with that system. I'm willing to bet that they also reward people who get the highest ratings.

Have one of your top executives return complaint calls. Give them the authority to make things right not only with that customer, but to institute procedures that will keep the problem from happening again.

I assume that this book is being read by high-level executives and managers. I do not need to go to great lengths to tell you how destructive negative word of mouth is. Please consider this just a friendly reminder to make sure that you have a way of encouraging complaints, monitoring them, and fixing their underlying causes. As Dick Cavett once said, "It's a rare man who wants to hear what he doesn't want to hear."

You should also be researching the kind of word of mouth that is going on about your company in the real world. If it's negative, you must take immediate steps to fix it.

How to Research Word of Mouth

It is extremely important to understand your customers' individual opinions, attitudes, and emotions—these are what drive their behavior. But it is not enough. In some ways, it is even more important to know the issues, concerns, and questions your prospects are actually *asking about* and how your customers *respond.*

Why? Because after hearing your sales pitch, or seeing your advertising, your prospects start *talking* about your product. As illustrated in Figure 8-1, word of mouth is what stands between your marketing input and the prospects' actual purchase.

Figure 8-1
Word of mouth stands between what you say and what your customers do.

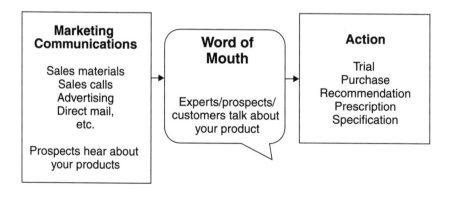

Your customers' private opinions about the product influence their *own* behavior. But what they *say* about the product influences the behavior of their friends and colleagues, which starts a ripple effect that ultimately determines the direction and speed of the marketplace.

Most companies spend huge amounts of money researching advertising, sales aids, and other promotional materials. Companies spend virtually no money *directly* researching word of mouth. The following indispensable questions too often go unanswered:

- What are the users willing to tell the nonusers?

- Exactly how do your customers describe your product?

- What are the nonusers willing to ask the users?

- What are the things they need to know, but are unwilling to ask?

- What happens when these issues are raised?

- Exactly what do your prospects have to know in order to trigger purchase?

- Exactly how do your customers answer the objections, concerns, and qualms of your prospects?

- How do your customers persuade their friends to use your product?

- How do your customers suggest they initially get to know (try) your product?

- What warnings, safeguards, tips, and suggestions do your customers suggest to your prospects?

- Are your sales messages, positioning, and important facts about your product getting through and surviving word of mouth?

■ Most importantly, what messages do you need to inject into the marketplace in order to turn the tide in your favor, and how will you deliver them?

Two Reasons Why Word-of-Mouth Research Is Essential

The first reason that word-of-mouth research is essential is that by being a "fly on the wall," you can hear the real attitudes underlying people's perceptions of your products as they talk about your product. There is no better way of getting to the underlying attitudes than inferring them from word of mouth. To be sure, not all attitudes are expressed in word of mouth. But you can almost always work backward and infer the underlying attitudes, beliefs, and opinions that are driving the word of mouth. In other words, you can go from word of mouth *back* to the attitudes driving them. You can't go forward, though, starting from the opinions, attitudes, and beliefs, and deduce what the word of mouth will be. This is because word of mouth is a live, interactive medium, and it depends as much on the questions of the recipients of word of mouth as it does on the willingness of the senders. In other words, just because the attitude is there, there is no guarantee that it will be expressed, or paid attention to.

The second reason to research word of mouth is actually to determine what the word of mouth itself is. Not only do you want to hear the contents of the word of mouth, you want to hear the sequence and the source. Often, sequence is as important as content. When things get a little out of sequence in word of mouth, people may say, "Wait a minute, you're losing me. Let's back up a little." In other marketing materials, when you've lost them, you've lost them.

Also, the source of the word of mouth is extremely important. In some situations, people won't try until they have heard the opinions of experts. In other situations, people feel that the experts are completely out of touch and will not understand their "ordinary" situation.

The only way to research word of mouth is to research it directly.

How to Design Word-of-Mouth Research

The usual way of researching word of mouth is to research it indirectly. People are asked to *recall* their word-of-mouth interactions—in surveys, for instance. To my knowledge, there is only one way to directly observe, and hear the *actual word of mouth in process*. I'm speaking of focus groups. The focus group, using designs described later in the chapter, is a way of causing actual word of mouth to happen, not just simulations of word of mouth. You can actually get customers talking with prospects in the process of convincing them. Dyads and triads also can be useful.

The Basic Research Model

The focus group must be tailored to the specific needs of word of mouth. The following is a basic research model, a template from which case-specific programs can be designed.

I caution you to use a professional moderator who specializes in this type of group. The reasons why can be found on the Qualitative Research Consultants Association Web site: www.qrca.org in a paper "Why Use a Professional Moderator?", which I wrote with extensive input from many other consultants.

This basic research design, called the 2-2-2 design by one of my clients, uses two focus groups of customers, two focus groups of prospects, and two of mixed groups of enthusiastic customers mixed with skeptical prospects. The first four groups can be alternated, starting with your customers or prospects, depending on the circumstances. Usually, it is best to start with customers. After the usual probing about attitudes and opinions of the product, they are asked questions like the following:

- What would you tell a friend?

- How would you persuade a skeptic?

■ What questions would you anticipate from a skeptic?

■ How would you answer their objections?

Your qualitative research consultant mentions the fact that she will be speaking with a group of skeptics soon, and asks them what they expect these people to say. The skeptical prospects are then given a description of the enthusiastic customer group, or played tape-recorded excerpts from that session. She explains the benefits of the product as described by the first group, as much as possible incorporating answers to the anticipated objections and turning them into benefits, so that they don't even come up. She then probes for the next level of qualms and objections. Always listening carefully for the first signs of persuasion, which may be someone saying, "Hmmm, that sounds interesting, I'll have to think about that." Notice that the person is not persuaded, but that her mind has been opened up.

The consultant keeps probing for objections that have been answered by the first group, but not accepted by the second group, or for new objections that haven't been answered. She tries out some of the answers that have been provided by your company, and some of her own, drawing upon her vast experience with similar situations.

Then she gets the next customer group to answer the objections, qualms, and questions that were expressed in the prospects' group. She has them discuss strategies and tactics for persuasion, and then tries these strategies and tactics in the next session. This may involve rewriting the concept statement, or simply describing the products based upon what was learned in the previous groups. By the end of the fourth session (the second prospects' session), the prospects are usually seriously interested in the product. Whereas you might have been able to anticipate some of the word of mouth that took place on both sides, you may be surprised by the *interaction between* the sides, which represents the real word of mouth.

Now you are ready for your word-of-mouth groups. These are the mixed groups of enthusiastic customers or product advocates, and skeptical prospects. The qualitative consultant could try to give the customers the assignment to "sell" the product to the prospects and assign the prospects to either resist or "unsell" the customers. This takes a very special sort of moderating that is a mixture of subtle guidance and devil's advocacy. The experienced moderator's instincts, coupled with what she learned in the first four groups, will usually tell her when to prod and provoke, and when to sit back and say nothing.

What you want to happen, ideally, is for the product advocates to persuade the skeptical prospects. Once you have that, *you know the ideal word of mouth that you want to encourage.* These strategies and tactics should serve as the basis of all your word-of-mouth efforts as well as advertising and sales messages.

By modifying this research design, you can put together experts with more typical customers, local influencers with their sphere of influence, retailers with their customers, and other kinds of people that you ordinarily wouldn't put together into focus groups because they tend to bias each other's opinions. Here, that is exactly what you want to observe! Any categories of people who are engaged in word of mouth can be researched in this way: auto mavens + car buyers, editors + their readers, medical specialists + general practitioners, physicians + nurses, travel agents + travelers, financial advisors + investors, and so on. Everyone except gladiators and lions, or cats and dogs.

For instance, you can survey new car buyers, asking why they bought their car and what is their current level of satisfaction. Or, you can run word-of-mouth research sessions to hear what they *actually* tell their friends. These are two completely different things, and you gain an enormous competitive advantage if you know both.

Telephone Focus Groups

The best way to conduct focus groups is to use *telephone focus groups*, a technique for bringing together hard-to-research people into group interviews via high-quality telephone conferencing equipment, from their own homes or offices, anywhere in the world. This advice will come as no surprise to those of you who know that I am the originator and developer of the telephone focus group. But I'm not recommending telephone groups for researching word of mouth because I developed them. I developed them because I needed a way of researching word of mouth.

Telephone focus groups allow you to put together people from different cities at the same time. This, in turn, allows people the psychological safety to be much more frank and open in their interactions.

As a rule, don't mix the kinds of people described above in face-to-face focus groups. There is too much chance of people either knowing each other in a given city or worrying that they will meet each other in a professional capacity. They will open up, however, in telephone groups. Also, you will find that you can recruit influential respondents who ordinarily wouldn't participate in research.

Telephone focus groups also tend to wipe out the distinctions introduced by differences in dress and other appearance factors. Often, people will accept an argument from a member of their own social class, but reject the same argument when offered by someone from a different class. In telephone focus groups, dress, ethnicity, facial expressions, and body language are irrelevant.

What to Do if You Don't Have "Users"

In the case of a new product, it is important to realize that word of mouth can—and should—be researched well before a product launch. Even before a product is introduced, there are often expectations about it. Many people, particularly innovators and early adopters, may have heard about the product and are discussing it. It is crucial that you know what's going on here. Even if they have not heard of your product, it is worth telling some people about it, not only to hear their reactions, as is so commonly done in focus groups, but also to hear how they would explain the product to colleagues. Often, they can come up with simple, elegant descriptions, metaphors, or analogies that people who are too close to the product cannot do in fewer than several pages.

With new products, instead of putting together users and nonusers, you want to put people who are extremely favorable to the product idea together with skeptics.

Other Research Designs
The Triangulation Design

In contrast to the 2-2-2 design, where you have users versus nonusers, the triangulation design uses different levels in the usage chain, such as salespeople, parents, and children, or distributors, retailers, and end users. This research model has been of particular use with pharmaceutical clients. During the launch of new medical products, I often conduct sessions of salespeople, physicians, and patients. I ask the salespeople what they have communicated to physicians, and then, in *separate* focus groups, ask the physicians what they have heard from the sales people. I also ask the physicians what they were too polite to ask the salespeople, and what was communicated to them that was not believed. Lastly, I ask them what they have heard from colleagues that does not jibe with what the salespeople have said.

I do the same thing with the patients, asking what their physician told them, what they believe, and whether they are complying with the physician's directions. I also ask them what other patients who have the same disease have said.

By getting people to report on what they were told and comparing it with what people think they heard, you can get important information.

Often what people hear is not what the other parties think they said, and what people think they said is often not what is actually heard. When there is this contradiction between the advocacy communication—for instance, between salespeople and physicians, or between physicians and patients—and the word-of-mouth communication (physician to physician, or patient to patient), it is almost invariably the word-of-mouth communication that is believed. Therefore, it is extremely important to identify discrepancies. These discrepancies can torpedo your marketing efforts. If the word of mouth is going one way and your salespeople, agents, dealers, or distributors are out in front of the stampede trying to turn it around, they will be trampled.

Don't forget that some of the most important word of mouth that you can have is among your salespeople (see Appendix C). If they are not fired up, they will not be behind your product, and customers will notice.

The Confrontation Design

In controversial situations, get all sides together and stand back! You may have to conduct separate sessions for the different sides, but you should get them together in telephone focus groups to hear how they interact with each other. Telephone groups tend to be less confrontational and more constructive. There has never been a fistfight in a telephone group!

The Expert/Opinion Leader/Peer Design.

Often, the information flows from experts, to opinion leaders, and then to peers. If you really want to understand the word of mouth in this kind of situation, you need to conduct sessions with experts, opinion leaders, and typical customers, then mix them together.

How to Analyze Word-of-Mouth Sessions

Word-of-mouth sessions should be analyzed from the standpoint of not only the actual word of mouth that is transmitted from person to person, but also its sequence, source, and appropriateness for where people are in the adoption cycle and the stages of the decision process.

When the word of mouth goes completely contrary to the positioning of the product, it is usually an urgent signal that the product needs to be repositioned. In only very rare cases can the word of mouth be turned around!

But beware of taking the word-of-mouth information literally. Enthusiastic customers will often improve the message of the marketing people, but they also can dangerously distort it, as for example when your customers niche your product too narrowly.

CHAPTER 9

Constructing a Word-of-Mouth Campaign

In the preceding chapters we have looked at:

- The elusive characteristics of word of mouth

- Its content and sources

- The sequence of word-of-mouth messages that move people through the decision process

- How to research word of mouth

We are now ready to construct word-of-mouth campaigns. Every campaign will be unique, depending upon the kind of product, the industry, the customers, and the nature of the competition. In order to succeed with a word-of-mouth campaign, you need:

- *A superior product,* or a product that is superior for a particular kind of person or situation. If you don't have product superiority, you need to create it.

- *A way of reaching* the key influencers in your marketplace.

- *A cadre of experts* who are willing to go to bat for you.

- And/or a large number of *enthusiastic customers* who can attest to how wonderful your product is.

- A way of reaching the *right prospects.*

- One or more *compelling stories* that people will want to tell to illustrate your product's superiority.

- A *way to substantiate*, prove, back up, or otherwise establish that your claims are true and will work out in the real world.

- A *way for people to have direct, low-risk experience* with your product, such as a demo, or a way of sampling.

- A *way of reducing overall risk,* such as an ironclad guarantee.

At this point, many people say, "If I had all these things, why would I need word of mouth?" Because these ingredients are just the raw ingredients of a successful marketing campaign. Having these by no means guarantees a successful product.

Furthermore, word of mouth is the most powerful way of delivering the truth. When the truth is on your side, the evidence is on your side. That means that people will have mostly positive experiences and, therefore, mostly positive things to say about it. Even the negatives will be put in context and balanced against the positives.

But it is up to you to organize, trigger, and harness word of mouth.

The "Ultimate" Word-of-Mouth Program

The ultimate word-of-mouth program is a technique that applies to high-ticket or high-volume products. Even if you don't have these kinds of products, it's still worth studying this ultimate form of word-of-mouth campaign because it is what we are trying to simulate for virtually all other kinds of campaigns. To get a clear understanding of what a word-of-mouth campaign can be, it is useful to learn how this particular one was invented, and to find out about some of its most successful applications.

This way of harnessing word of mouth was developed in the pharmaceutical industry. But don't think for a moment that it applies only to physicians. In some ways, the pharmaceutical industry is the most difficult to operate in. As the old saying goes, "if you can make it here, you can make it anywhere." This model has in fact been extremely effective in a wide variety of industries, with a wide variety of people.

How I First Harnessed Word of Mouth

I invented and developed the telephone focus group around 1970. It allowed me access to hard-to-reach, geographically dispersed, high-level people and—more importantly—to mix them together in unusual ways to learn about the word of mouth among them.

One of the most useful combinations was putting the first few enthusiastic users of a product together with skeptics, to see how the users would attempt to convince their less enthusiastic peers. Their wording, logic, and sequencing could then be used in promotional materials.

An amazing thing happened: *Even when the users were vastly outnumbered, they almost always convinced the nonadopters to try, or retry, the product.* Even one or two would convince ten or twelve! We followed up and found that most participants had in fact tried, and then bought (or started prescribing), the product.

Most people have noticed this phenomenon in focus groups, and much has been written about it, mostly in the form of criticism of the focus group technique—the old "one person can bias a whole group" criticism. However, one man's *bias* is another man's *finding.* Let me explain.

When people change their minds, you have a momentous event. People don't change their beliefs easily. In fact, they go to war defending their beliefs! It's important to understand exactly what got people to change their minds because whatever it is (a rational argument, an emotional appeal, a belief, experience, opinion, fear, hope, etc.) it's either an opportunity or a threat. If it turns out predictably to turn people toward your product, you have an opportunity. If it sways people against your product, you have a vulnerability. You want to know why and how it was done, so that it can be duplicated or defused. I kept looking at this group-persuasion phenomenon and made two additional discoveries: It only happened under certain circumstances, and it was virtually always one way: *adopters, no matter how few, convinced nonadopters, no matter how many.* There was an extraordinary amount of constructive, respectful experience sharing going on, rather than abstract discussion, disagreement, or debate. It was as if the nonadopters wanted to be convinced.

My partner Ron Richards (Ron is now an independent marketing consultant in San Francisco. He is president of ResultsLab and part of our network of consultants.) and I knew that there was a powerful force at work. We quickly rejected the idea that it was "peer pressure," because the *minority* was swaying the *majority.* This force was working *despite* peer pressure. In one of our discussions late into the night, we had an epiphany: The force that was causing this amazing phenomenon to happen was word of mouth.

People were in an open situation in which they were free to learn from their peers, uninfluenced by outside forces. Since "you can't argue with success," even one successful person would sway a whole group! The main difference between what we were doing and ordinary word of mouth was that we had caused it to happen, predictably, on a budget and on a schedule. We had turned it into a medium. *We had harnessed word of mouth.*

It's Even Better Than Ordinary Word of Mouth

There were other differences between what we were doing and ordinary word of mouth. Most word of mouth, studies have shown, is negative. Our moderator, while not injecting information and not exerting influence, could bring up important points that the participants might have left unexamined, or turn the conversation to a more constructive direction by asking for solutions to problems. If the moderator at any time lost neutrality and took an advocacy position, the entire atmosphere of the group was poisoned and the objective examination and experience sharing stopped.

Of course, once the research was accomplished, we couldn't run more groups under the guise of research, just to increase sales. We went to Roche (one of our clients), from whose focus groups we had developed many insights, and explained the conflict to its management. We proposed a very simple solution: full disclosure. We would invite physicians to groups in which no reference to marketing research was made. The sessions would be described as exactly what they were: open discussions in which physicians could discuss the drug in question with other physicians who had had success with it, sponsored by the manufacturer of the drug in the hope that once physicians heard how other people were using it successfully, they would also use it successfully.

Roche agreed to fund a large number of telephone conference sessions on Laradopa®, their brand of L-dopa, an anti-Parkinson's Disease drug that was a very difficult product to market. (It was the drug whose story was dramatically told in the movie *Awakenings.*) On introduction, its sales had skyrocketed, only to disappoint because of its many side effects. Sales tumbled. The difficulty in using it was finding the ideal dosage that would correct the symptoms that appeared with too little medicine, and avoiding the side effects brought on by too much medicine. For most patients, there was a mixture of symptoms and side effects. Many physicians had tried it and dropped it because of their frustrations in trying to use it. As one physician put it, "The symptoms of Parkinson's Disease are blamed on God. The side effects of medication are blamed on me."

We scheduled many telephone conference sessions, each with a combination of well-chosen people: Eight primary care physicians who treated large numbers of Parkinson's patients without L-dopa, a couple of physicians who treated with L-dopa, and a neurologist who was an expert in using the drug. Sales increased sixfold almost immediately. It was clear that the about-face in the doctors' prescription choices was due to our sessions. This was the first use of word-of-mouth sessions, a stunning success by any measure.

What Actually Goes On in the Sessions?

Usually, there are about ten people, all of them participating by telephone, at home in the evening, from all across the country. The sessions take place over a custom-built telephone conference system. They are extremely informal, with participation in the form of questions and discussion. Often we poll the group to find out what topics, questions, issues, or concerns are the most important to them. Then the guest expert talks for a few minutes to provide general background, answering the questions brought up in the beginning of the session. Specific cases may also be discussed. Sessions usually last an hour, but an hour on the phone is equivalent to at least an hour and a half face to face.

The sessions are designed from both an educational and marketing perspective. They are tested and tuned, so that they are appealing, informative, and of genuine help to the participants in translating information into decisions, and decisions into action. Then, and only then, should the client commit to dozens, or even hundreds, of sessions.

There is no set formula. You have to know what you are doing. Each product is unique, each program is unique, each session is unique, and each participant is unique. Session and program design are, therefore, of paramount importance. You need to avoid the trap of programs that have wonderful educational value, but that do not further the marketing objectives. Programs must supply the critical information people need in order to overcome the basic resistance to using the product. Avoid programs that may meet the marketing objectives perfectly but that are so transparently self-serving and promotional that people are offended. Just as you can't throw "selling points" on a page and automatically expect to have an effective ad, and just as you can't merely recite benefits to a person and expect that a sales call will be effective, you can't throw together groups and expect effective word-of-mouth sessions.

Success Stories of Word-of-Mouth Sessions

Since 1970, we've conducted more than 6000 groups of people in the process of deciding on products and services: executives, physicians, managers, salespeople, agents, distributors, farmers, and ordinary consumers. So, I've heard tens of thousands of people in the process of engaging in word of mouth as they decided on an incredibly wide variety of products. In addition, I've either conducted or listened to thousands of expert sessions, customer seminars, advisory groups, sales groups, "peer influence" groups, and other sessions in which I could hear word of mouth in action. I've conducted groups of product enthusiasts, product rejecters, and people who were hostile to products.

These sessions have been both a fishbowl and a laboratory, rolled into one. It's been a way to observe, and to experiment with how word of mouth speeds up and influences the customer decision process.

Several of these word-of-mouth campaigns have caused record-breaking sales increases. To this day, some of my clients still won't give me permission to talk about them because they regard my techniques as a secret weapon. I can, however, reveal the insights into how to use word of mouth to accelerate the customers' decision process and how to influence it to go in your favor.

In the pharmaceutical industry alone I have seen sales increases of 300 to 1500 percent and more in dozens of programs. One product had a 1 percent market share that was flat. It seemed that nothing could sell it. A year later, through a word-of-mouth campaign, sales jumped to 36 percent market share, and are still climbing as of this writing. It's the market leader, by far.

Another product's sales jumped from a little less than $100 million to more than a $1 billion in a year, and are still climbing. This happened after doing only ten sessions with the critical opinion leaders. The entire marketplace was just waiting for permission to use the product, which the sessions provided, triggering perhaps the biggest word-of-mouth avalanche in pharmaceutical history.

Word of Mouth Is Now a "Medium"

We realized that we had turned word of mouth from an out-of-control force into a promotional medium, something that could be included in the promotional mix: It was budgetable, deliverable on a schedule, and predictable. In a lot of ways, it was more measurable than other media: We know exactly who had participated and could measure the subsequent prescriptions. Because it was done by telephone conference, we could reach people worldwide without the limits of geography, and include experts from anywhere without making them travel.

We also realized that we had invented something more than just another promotional gimmick. It is as basic as salespeople, advertising, and sales promotion. Each major element of the promotional mix delivers something that customers need in order to make their decisions. The basic need that advertising meets is to reach large numbers of people efficiently. Salespeople deliver custom-made messages interactively. Peer word-of-mouth sessions deliver experience needed for verification and confirmation.

Word-of-Mouth Sessions Are a Solid Marketing Tool

Word-of-mouth sessions have become a major promotional item in many products' budgets, in some cases causing deep slashes in the amount of money spent on salespeople, advertising, direct mail, and sampling. They have also been measured to be the most effective selling method for many products—again, more effective than sales-people, advertising, direct mail, and sampling. It's clear that word-of-mouth sessions are a major addition to the marketing mix and are here to stay, because they increase sales cost-effectively. When done right, they are the most professional, honest, and persuasive means of communicating with high-level people, such as physicians, executives, and other hard-to-reach and hard-to-influence people.

Making the Sessions More Valuable

In the last decade, "Peer Influence" or "Peer Selling" groups have grown enormously. But most of them are done face to face, in the mistaken belief that people prefer them that way. Surveys and real-world tests show that people—despite the fact that they may indicate on surveys that they prefer face-to-face sessions—tend actually to accept and show up for telephone sessions more than they do for face-to-face sessions, provided that certain conditions are met.

The key is building in and communicating the educational value of the sessions.

How do you structure the best programs? First, approach the program as if it were a product, which it is. With a product, you figure out:

- What people's perceived needs are

- How to position the product

- What benefits to emphasize in what order

- How to communicate them

Similarly, with these sessions you need to find out, through client discussions and focus groups, what the customers and prospects need to learn in order to effectively use the product. Then ask, "How will they best learn these things?" You can't just tell them, because telling is not teaching, and teaching is not learning. Then design and structure a customer-driven program (in this case the participants are the customers as much as the clients).

You must figure out what the participants need to learn, in what sequence, from what sources, and in what form. You can design study materials for review before the sessions and handouts during and after the sessions, via a private site on the Internet, or via mailings to people beforehand. Sometimes the sessions have to contain experts, sometimes only peers, and sometimes there is a need for a follow-up session. Much of this is governed by keeping in mind the basic function of word of mouth: accelerating the spread of experience. Pay particular attention to what experience has to be shared, and what will be the most efficient and meaningful way to do this. Sessions for different types of people have to be built in, with flexible, but well thought-out agendas.

The Power of Follow-Up Sessions

The most important next step after telephone word-of-mouth session is the follow-up session. In a word-of-mouth session, participants learn a lot, but there is no follow-up to their learning. They have no way to reinforce their learning, to put their experiences in context, to correct mistakes, and to explore other issues. Programs offering participants one session are effective, but when participants are offered the opportunity to apply their experience and come back to a follow-up session, their product usage multiplies.

Remember that the major function of word of mouth is broadening one's base of experience. After the initial session, there is experience going on that isn't shared. With two sessions—the second one following up the experience gained from the first session—there is a multiplication of the confidence gained by the shared additional experience. This translates into increased usage. In several studies, the participants in the initial sessions increased usage threefold, but the usage of people who had participated in both initial sessions and follow-up sessions increased an average of *tenfold*.

How to Move the "Late Adopters"

People who characterize themselves as late adopters, or even laggards, are often among the first to try a product when they have the support of this kind of a system. Often people are slow to adopt because it is their personal policy to wait to see what the experience of others is. But when they are offered the chance to try the product under low-risk conditions, and are allowed to evaluate their trial in the context of others' experience, they frequently jump at the chance. So it is naïve to pigeonhole people rigidly as innovators, early adopters, middle majority, late adopters, and laggards. These are useful categories, as we have seen, but people can break out of their category. If you know how to create the conditions that give people the right support, you can get people who would ordinarily have taken three to five years to adopt a product, to adopt it in a matter of a few weeks or months.

Maintaining Objectivity

Candidly, I'm very worried about the future of this medium. Experience has already shown that there have been abuses, just as there have been abuses of other media. However, peer word-of-mouth sessions are in some ways more subject to abuse. No one expects a salesperson, or an ad, or a brochure to be objective. After all, they are advocacy sources. That's why word of mouth is needed, to give fair balance. So, anything that compromises fair balance and objectivity strikes at the heart of what people are looking for and will backfire in word-of-mouth sessions. It is very easy to lose objectivity, to play down one issue and emphasize another. The moderator can forget his or her role as the guardian of fair balance, openness, and thorough examination of the evidence. The expert can become overly enthusiastic. The moderator can give a sales pitch. There are many ways to lose the sense of being a disinterested party, and all of them hurt the program, the product, and the medium. All of them can ultimately backfire, and all of them make it less likely that the person will participate in the future.

Fortunately, in another sense, word-of mouth sessions are the hardest medium to abuse. It is live. People can and will object if statements are biased, and they will bring things back on track. It's hard to hide the truth in an open forum. These kinds of sessions, properly run, are the most honest form of marketing.

Situations That Benefit from Word-of-Mouth Programs

There are many marketing situations that don't respond well to conventional approaches, no matter how creative. The following situations can usually benefit from word-of-mouth sessions:

- *When there are credibility problems.* If people don't believe your claims, they usually don't believe your evidence either. Word of mouth provides believable independent corroboration.

- *When there are breakthroughs.* Breakthroughs require departures from present thinking and practice. Most people wait for other people to provide this key validation.

- *When there are marginal improvements (where people are reluctant to use something new for only a little improvement).* Here, peers can show that the little differences make a big difference in practical applications.

- *Where the product has to be tried in large numbers or over time.* The process can often be accelerated by word-of-mouth seminars where there are trials, and where the experience is collected and shared.

- *Where there is high risk in trying the product.* The risk can often be reduced, shared, or put into perspective by talking with peers.

■ *With older or mature products that have a new story that people tend to ignore.* Again, peer discussion can get people to take a new view.

■ *With unfair competitive practices, such as spreading rumors, or telling lies about your product.* This is uncontrolled word of mouth at its worst. The right combination of experts and peers can set the record straight.

■ *When there are governmental or other restrictions on what you may say or claim directly.* Experts can often say things that you may not say or claim directly.

Products with Which to Avoid Word-of-Mouth Sessions

■ "Me-too" products where a seminar would not provide meaningful added value.

■ Products that can't be tried and where there is no consensus among experts.

■ Products that are clearly inferior, without having a compensating superiority for a particular application.

■ Products that are so much a matter of personal taste or emotion that rational discussion is irrelevant to the decision.

■ Products where the decision value is so small (low price/low volume) that the medium will not be cost-effective. On the other hand, high price/low volume or low price/high volume products are often ideal. The principle here is that there has to be enough value in the decision to justify what the program will cost. However, there may be times when the program is not justified by the amount that the participants can purchase, prescribe, or directly recommend, but where they are influential enough to start a word-of-mouth chain that more than justifies the program

CHAPTER 10

Word of Mouth, the "Tried and True" Way

In a recent interview on word of mouth and referral selling, I was asked a very provocative question. The interviewer had just heard about word-of-mouth sessions, and wanted to look at more ordinary products and businesses where they don't apply. He said, "Let's imagine that you own a local ski store. How would you advise the owner of that ski store to use word of mouth when he doesn't have one specific product he wants to sell and where he can't afford the kinds of word-of-mouth sessions you have been describing?"

Well, it just so happens that I have experience in a similar situation. I'll describe it, draw principles from the example, and then address the ski store question directly.

My Father's Drugstore

My father was a brilliant marketer. I grew up in his various drugstores, and watched as he took stores that he had picked up for a song, and turned them into cash cows. He owned the largest volume drugstore in Brooklyn, New York, and later the largest independent drugstore in Manhattan, both of which started out as small stores. He would typically buy a store that was filling about ten prescriptions per day, and in a few months that store would be filling *hundreds* of prescriptions per day.

He did it almost exclusively by using word of mouth.

The first thing he did was to give customers something worth talking about. After all, a drugstore is a drugstore. They all have more or less the same merchandise, and certainly their prescriptions are absolutely standard. When a physician writes a prescription, it should be filled in exactly the same way by every drugstore in the United States. This was especially true years ago when there were very few generic drugs and when substituting drugs was illegal.

So the first thing my father did was to provide an extraordinary level of service. For instance, he was free with advice and recommendations for new and superior products. And he would go to any lengths to get an unusual item that a customer requested, instead of saying that he didn't carry the item. He bought in large quantities, sometimes pooling buying power with friends in other parts of the city, passing the savings along to customers. He always priced his prescriptions substantially lower than any drugstore in the neighborhood, remembered his customers names, treated them with respect and courtesy, made them feel special, and in general catered to them in a way that went beyond their immediate financial worth to him.

The first customers to come to a new store were especially favored. He would ask them where they were from and where they worked. He would tell them how his store was now different under new management. He was always ready with some kind of convincer—a special deal or a free gift—that he had up his sleeve (he was also a magician). He'd ask them what medications they were taking, and quote them a good price (privately he used to call it a "come-back price"). This was especially true if he saw a word-of-mouth opportunity. For instance, if the person worked for a large company, or lived in a large apartment building, he would give them a special price on their medications and tell them that he was doing so in the hope that they would pass the good word about the store on to their friends.

He would be willing even to lose money on a customer who brought him many other customers. He had people coming in with handfuls of prescriptions that they were getting filled for their friends.

Here are the principles that we can draw from my father's example:

Give Them Something Worth Talking About

If people have better things to talk about than your product or service, that's what they will talk about. You have to give them something special to tell their friends and colleagues.

Cater to Your Initial Customers Shamelessly

Especially cater to those who are major potential sources of word of mouth. It doesn't matter if you lose money on them; it is the word-of-mouth stream, and thereby the revenue stream they create, that is important. These first customers are the early adopters of the product or service. Their direct revenues may not be particularly great in and of themselves. But these first customers might lead to hundreds or thousands of other customers eventually. Spare no efforts in cultivating them.

Give Them Incentives to Engage in Word of Mouth

If there are rewards and incentives to encourage them to engage in word of mouth, they are much more likely to be willing to tell their friends about your product or service. Give them a reward, discount, or other incentive for bringing in a friend. Give the incentive to both the referrer and the person referred.

Ask for Their Word of Mouth

The best way to get someone to do something is to ask them. But don't ask them to do you a favor, ask *them to do their friends a favor* by recommending you. Most direct requests read like this: "Please tell your friends about our wonderful service." But better phrases are "Please do your friends a favor by recommending us" or "Who else do you know who could benefit from our extraordinary service?"

By the way, whom else do you know who would benefit from this book? They might appreciate it if you took a moment to e-mail them a recommendation. You might want to point out to them how important word of mouth is to their product, and how this book will open their eyes to the possibilities of dramatically increasing their sales while cutting their marketing budget.

If there is a company whose product you particularly like and want to be successful—even if you don't know someone there—you might try e-mailing the marketing vice president or president and tell them how this book will make their product even more successful.

(Almost) Everything I Know about Marketing I Learned in My Father's Drugstore, or Irving Silverman's Rules of Marketing

I went to work in my father's drugstore when I was nine years old, as a stockboy, progressing to cashier, clerk, and pharmacist's assistant. Retailing is a high-feedback environment in which you can see the effects of what you are doing quickly. You count the money at the end of each day, count the prescriptions, and see the faces of customers. I later became a psychologist and a marketing consultant, but realized that what I had learned back in my father's drugstore, particularly about word of mouth, applies to every business and every product—not exactly in the form I learned it, but translated into a form appropriate to the particular circumstances. Treat this section as allegorical. If there is a lesson that follows that you think is irrelevant to your product, your business, or your job, I urge you to pay particular attention to it: It is likely to be one you are neglecting at your peril. I like to think my father would have been proud that the lessons he taught were put to good use.

Here then is a collection of universal marketing truisms that we all too often forget.

■ Rule one: The customer is always right. Rule two: In the rare cases where you *know* the customer is *really* wrong, refer to rule one.

■ Don't approach the customer with the intention of selling something. Instead, politely ask the customer, "How can I help you?"

■ Always tell the truth, and tell the whole truth. Never withhold the disadvantages of a product, even one you are enthusiastic about.

■ There's always a way to tell the truth, even if the Board of Pharmacy or the FDA won't let you. For example, there was a law against advertising lower prescription prices, and my father was discounting prescriptions. He was frustrated that he couldn't put a sign on his window telling customers that his prices were lower. I suggested that he put up a sign with the text of the relevant law, together with a statement of his disapproval of the law, figuring that the customers would get the message. He did something better: He put up a simple sign that said, "Let us price your current prescription." The Board of Pharmacy made it clear informally that it didn't like it, but it couldn't do anything to stop him.

■ Always surprise the customers by giving them a little more than they expected.

■ Give them a reason to buy, or many reasons to buy, not only in your place of business, but from you personally. Make them come back and refuse to be waited on by anyone other than you.

■ Make eye contact. Say it with a smile, even over the telephone, but make sure it's a real smile.

■ Find a lot of little ways to make doing business with you a little better: Give a warmer greeting, provide a nicer floor, better lighting, a better bag, extra matches, faster service, free delivery, lower prices, more selection. There are always scores of ways to increase value. Write them on little scraps of paper. Your pockets should be bulging from them (my father's were).

■ Never be annoyed when a customer asks you to change a large bill, or gives you pennies, even if he doesn't buy anything. Someday he will. Always check to make sure that you give the correct change.

■ The customer is not an annoyance taking you away from your real work. He or she is your reason for being.

■ Get a mental picture of the customer walking past your competitor to come to you. Never take him for granted, never rely on habit, because one day he will go in to try the competitor (if for nothing more than variety) and never come back. Always ask, "What have I done for him lately?"

■ Always dust off a dusty bottle or box, but never let the customer see you do it.

■ Never, ever, in any way embarrass a customer, especially by making him feel ignorant.

■ Never answer a question coming from a desire to show how smart you are. Answer the question, but come from a desire to help the customer make the best decision. Make him feel smart for asking the question.

■ Never shout across the store the following words, or their equivalent: "How much are these condoms?"

■ When you don't know, say so. Never make things up and

don't speculate about what the answer might be. Find out the answer on the spot, or promise to find out. Do whatever you have to do to find out, no matter whom you have to ask, whom you have to call. Call the president of the company if you have to, and don't let her off the hook either.

■ Every customer is special. Get to know them. They're fascinating. Call every customer by name. If you don't know the name, ask for it again and again if necessary, with a self-deprecating joke. They may think you have a bad memory, but will never think you don't think they are special.

■ Never let a customer walk, for any reason. Meet any price, even if you don't believe the customers. So what if you have to fill their prescriptions at cost. Maybe that's the price you have to pay to sell them their cosmetics.

■ On the other hand, don't let known shoplifters into the store. Shoplifters want stores in which the clerks neglect them. So, don't neglect customers.

■ Act as though every moment a customer is waiting, he is thinking bad thoughts about you. Don't ever let two clerks or pharmacists talk when a customer is waiting. The worst thing you can do is count your money while you keep a customer waiting. Nobody has so much money that they can't afford to lose count and start counting over again.

■ Remember that no matter how much they like you, they buy the product because they want it or need it. They pay you money because what they are getting is worth more to them than the cash they give you. If you can suggest something better, without pressuring them, they will probably be grateful. Giving them a sample may cost you a present sale, but it's worth it. Sometimes it's helpful to ask a simple question like "We've been selling a lot of X lately, and people have been coming back for more. I'm curious, have you tried it, and what do you think?" Always respect the fact that it's their choice.

■ Never pressure anyone into anything. The best that you can do under those circumstances is make the sale at the risk of losing the customer.

■ Never knowingly give bad advice. In fact, generally stay away from giving any kind of advice. Just help people come to the right decision.

■ Personally visit any store a customer compliments, particularly competitors' stores that are beating your prices, even if it's an hour's ride into another part of the city. That storeowner is probably doing a whole bunch of things that you can do even better. If the competitor knows you, send in other people to report back to you. (I didn't know this was called marketing research. These were my first marketing research assignments.)

■ Hire a shopping service to prepare periodic reports on the pricing and inventory of your competitors, as well as on how your people are treating customers (mystery shopping services).

■ If you hear of a store where the management is insulting customers, buy it. You'll buy it for a song, since the management will be in trouble due to negative word of mouth. Just putting up a sign "Under New Management" will increase sales dramatically. Then, if you don't want it, sell it based on the increased sales. (My father bought and sold dozens of stores.)

■ Look where the leverage is. One physician or office nurse who is convinced you are better brings hundreds of customers and their friends though word of mouth (I didn't know at the time to call them leveraged influencers).

■ Always look for ways to build the business. Start with finding ways to "make a stranger a customer."

■ There is an old adage that the three most important things in determining the worth of a store are location, location, and location. On the other hand, don't forget that most people, even wealthy people, will walk several blocks to save a dollar, or see a smile, or be treated right.

■ Always run a sale or a promotion or an offbeat event. Make them keep coming back, even if for nothing else than to see what you are up to next.

■ Use the best sign-maker you can find and pay him more than anybody else. Plaster your windows with his signs, but not before you check his spelling.

■ If someone is mad at you, they will tell everyone who will listen for as long as they are angry, maybe even longer. If they are satisfied, they have better things to talk about, such as who else they are mad at. So, correct any dissatisfaction, no matter how small, and ask customers to send their friends. Nothing beats word of mouth.

■ Treat your employees, and salespeople who sell to you, the same way you treat your customers.

■ When filling a prescription, or doing anything else which could have terrible consequences if a mistake is made, don't make mistakes. Ever. Put in a zero error system. Figure out a way to make it foolproof. With a prescription, the person filling it is never the one to put it away. The bottle is left on top of the prescription. Someone else checks to see that they match before putting the bottle back on the shelf and putting the prescription in the file. Occasionally, put the wrong bottle on the prescription to make sure it is caught.

■ Always measure your performance. In a drugstore, make a chart of the number of prescriptions filled per day and the gross volume of the store per day. Keep a running average. No matter how good a job you think you are doing, if these two measures are not going up significantly, you are doing a lousy job.

■ Always ask the customer to "Come back soon."

▪ If customers say they are moving away, offer to fill their prescriptions by mail.

▪ Make jokes. Lots of them. Only a serious person can make good jokes. (As Zero Mostel said, "Humor is just a funny way of being serious.")

▪ *Non bastardi carborundum.* Don't let bastards wear you down.

That's all. Come back soon.

Specific Steps in Creating a Word-of-Mouth Campaign

First, you need a group of product enthusiasts. If you have them, you need to take steps to identify exactly who they are. If you don't have them, you must create them. Here's how:

Seed the Market

Get the product into the hands of key influencers any way you can. This might include giving away your product to the first dozen or two dozen customers. Netscape gave out its Navigator program to millions of people to become the market leader. Then Microsoft took it away by using the same methods.

What do you do with products that cost a half million dollars? You can't give them away. You put the product out for indefinite loan or demo, perhaps on a rotating basis. But you must *find some way of getting the product into the hands of key influencers.*

For financial products, what do you do? After all, you can't give away free insurance policies or free mutual fund shares! You *can* give away planning kits, CD-ROMs, tracking services on a Web site, etc. When you can't give away product samples, seed the market with *useful* surrogates that will showcase your product.

The idea here is that you have to *get experts and key influencers fired up about your product.* The key influencers do not have to be luminaries or well-known experts. They can be simply the people who tend to use products first and who tend to influence their peers.

Then, *provide a means of transmission* for the pent-up word of mouth that these people have. They *want* to talk with their colleagues and friends about the product. But when they see these people, they might talk about something completely different from your product, even though they would rave about your product if they were asked. So, like all other marketing elements, *you need a channel of delivery.*

Deliver Word of Mouth

There are many channels for the delivery of word of mouth, ranging from the conventional to the more creative methods.

Use Testimonials and Endorsements. You can capture *testimonials and endorsements* and put them in your promotional materials. This is an extremely powerful device that is used often, but not often enough (except in the front of every paperback book, where it is used too much). How many times have you seen an actor in an ad saying things that would be so much better said by a real customer?

A CASE IN POINT

There is a bank in New York, the Anchor Savings Bank, that has radio commercials of real customers raving about how well they were treated. They sound "terrible," with heavy ethnic accents and poor grammar, except that there can be no doubt that these are real people who believe every poorly articulated word they are uttering. It is among the most credible advertising that I have ever heard.

The Customer Referral Selling System. Another way to deliver word of mouth is to develop a *customer referral selling system.* You can get referrals from your initial customers. Again, the power of referral selling is well known, but it is neglected in many more instances than it is used. In Chapter 12, we will discuss how to set up a customer referral system.

Get More Creative. The methods mentioned above are powerful and underutilized, but they are still well within the boundaries of conventional marketing, and you might already be using them. (Still, you are probably not using them frequently or creatively enough.) But now let's push the envelope a little:

1. Form an ongoing advisory group that you bring together once a year at a resort, but once a month by teleconference, or daily by list group.

2. Form an ongoing group of typical customers.

3. Create *events* that bring users together and invite nonusers. Saturn, Harley-Davidson, and Lexus have been particularly successful with this approach.

4. Produce *cassettes, videotapes,* and *clips* on your Web *site* featuring enthusiastic customers talking with other enthusiastic customers. Find a way of delivering these to prospects. The new medium is CDs that you custom-create for each potential customer.

5. Conduct *seminars* in which customers and/or experts talk with interested prospects. These can be done face-to-face or by teleconference. The seminar is the most powerful method of harnessing and delivering word of mouth. It is truly a medium: It can be scheduled, budgeted, managed, and predicted better than most other media. It is particularly relevant for products where people consult trusted advisors, such as doctors, lawyers, financial advisors, or accountants.

6. Develop a referral selling system. (Explained in detail in Chapter 12.)

Put Principles into Action

Let's take the ski store mentioned previously as a case study. Regard the example as allegorical. It applies not only to all types of retail establishments, but also to any type of business that deals with large numbers of people. It even applies to whole product lines. Use it to stretch your thinking.

The object of a word-of-mouth campaign is to get people talking with their friends about what a wonderful "shop" you have. Here is what a word-of-mouth program might look like:

- **An affiliation program.** Form a ski club, or otherwise make people a member of an inner circle of preferred customers. Issue cards or stickers and give people member benefits mostly centering on word-of-mouth referrals. Memberships would entitle them to discounts and various events.

- **Events.** Hold a seminar on how to ski better. Use video showings, speakers, and demos in the store and on the slopes. Give priority to word-of-mouth referrals.

- **A specific word-of-mouth appeal in every communication.** Put handouts into bags and pass out flyers that mention the kind of store you have, what you stand for, and why you are different from all other stores. Make a direct appeal to tell a friend. Offer special incentives to tell friends, such as a discount for both the customer and the friend.

- **Testimonials.** Use endorsements from well-known skiers.

- **Internet.** Set up an Internet site with a discussion group and an "ask the expert" (you) Q & A session.

- **The outrageous.** Do at least one outrageous thing each day that could generate word of mouth. Send some of these items to the local paper. For instance, a restaurant gives away all food during the main dinner hour on a random Monday, its slowest day. But no one knows which Monday! Why not cut $200 off your ad budget and give away a random set of skis every month?

■ **Empowerment.** Empower employees to do over-the-top things, especially to turn around a dissatisfied customer.

■ **Advisory group.** Form an advisory group of particularly plugged-in customers. Meet with them for a half hour to an hour by conference call every month or two. They can advise you about what new products they have seen or what promotions you can run.

■ **Network.** Use your own word of mouth to network with other ski store owners on a regular basis. Set up a regular conference call or Internet discussion group with non-competitive forward-thinking people like yourself in other cities. You can tell each other what new products are hot, or brainstorm ideas for bringing in new customers and selling more equipment to current customers. Don't underestimate the power of your own peer word of mouth.

■ **Special sales.** Run sales that are for preferred customers only, but allow those customers to bring a friend. Therefore, the entire sale is by word-of-mouth referral only.

■ **Testimonials.** Enclose testimonials from real customers in all ads and promotional materials.

■ **Referrals.** Ask for referrals. Ask people for the names of their friends to add to your mailing list. Base the appeal on the notion that by telling them about limited special offers not generally advertised, they are doing their friends a favor.

■ **Script.** Tell people exactly what to say in their word-of-mouth communication. For instance "Tell your friends about our superior service."

How many businesses actually implement a word-of-mouth-driven marketing program with even some of these obvious elements? None of these ideas is particularly hard to implement. None of them alone will have a dramatic effect. But when many of them are put together, critical mass is reached, and the store will have an explosion of new business in a surprisingly short amount of time. Every skier in the area will start to hear about the store from many people and sources. They may not even be conscious of how many times they have heard of the store. But when they pass by, or when they are about to purchase equipment, the name of the store will pop into their heads, along with the thought that "I've been hearing good things about that store, I think I'll try it."

Build these kinds of word-of-mouth activities into your business. Many of these are the sorts of things that are basic, known to be powerful, and almost always neglected. As a bare minimum, every business should try to:

■ Find out where every lead comes from.

■ Ask every customer and prospect, "Who else could benefit from our services?"

■ Institute a formal referral system.

■ Actively collect testimonials and use them.

■ Create a customer advisory group.

■ Identify and maintain contact with the opinion leaders.

CHAPTER 11

Campaign Methods That Work Best

Word-of-Mouth Campaigns with High-Ticket, Professional Products

Word of mouth among business people and professionals (such as physicians, pharmacists, architects, and financial advisors) is very different from word of mouth for relatively low-ticket consumer products. The more expensive and complicated a product is, the more word of mouth comes into play. This is true because these products are more risky in terms of time, money, and potential damage to professional reputation. High-ticket products are not as easily tried as simple consumer products. People have to rely on other people's experience to substitute for all or part of the experience they would get in a trial. Here is what a word of mouth program might look like for such a product:

Experts' Word-of-Mouth Sessions

First get the experts on your side by bringing them into conferences, seminars, advisory groups, and the like. Use the people who helped develop and test the product to spread the word among these people. For instance, with a new medication, the clinical investigators should be put together with other experts and medical specialists. The investigators can describe the clinical studies and their personal experiences with the drug before it hits the market. They can also explain things in relevant and powerful terms, far beyond what the experts can get by reading clinical studies.

Spreading the Word

Now that the experts are on board, and solidly behind your product, you want to have them *spread the word to the next tier of influencers.* Encourage them to write articles and papers, as well as grant interviews and the like, to spread the word. Give them slide shows. You also want to include them in seminars, workshops, symposia, and forums. Increasingly, various forms of teleconferencing and online services are being used for this, although the simplest, most convenient, and most personal medium is still the basic audio teleconference.

Experts' Roundtables

Another way of getting expert opinion across to the early adopters is to distribute *experts' roundtables* via print, videotape, or audio-cassette. They can be printed in industry journals, or made into stand-alone reprints. The easiest way to produce an experts' roundtable is by audio teleconference.

After conducting countless focus groups to try to determine which of these modes people prefer, I have come to the conclusion that it is a matter of personal style and learning preferences. No one method is superior. You should produce materials in a variety of modes. For instance, people who have long commutes like to listen to audiotapes. Giving them a videotape might be completely useless. Some people don't like to participate live with other people, so they may refuse invitations to audio teleconferences, symposia, and dinner meetings.

You want to make your advertising and sales efforts support, encourage, and piggyback on the word of mouth. Put endorsements, testimonials, and references to papers into your advertising. Have your salespeople mention what other customers have been saying about the product. Have them put customers in touch with satisfied customers. Get people's permission to use them as references. Most people won't call, but the mere citing of a reference is extremely powerful in itself.

Which Word-of-Mouth Methods Work Best?

As you have probably guessed, there is no one particular word-of-mouth method that works best in every circumstance. Some of the least effective in one kind of situation work spectacularly well in other circumstances. Often, the least effective applicable word-of-mouth method can create more sales than the best of the other marketing methods. Word of mouth is simply in a different league from advertising, sales, or promotions. Figure 11-1 illustrates the relative credibility of word-of-mouth delivery methods.

Here follows a listing of the word-of-mouth delivery methods, ranked roughly from most to least effective. Obviously, there are exceptions. Remember that we are talking about a word-of-mouth *campaign* here. Since you should be using as many of these elements as you can, ranking may be irrelevant. In decreasing order, with the most influential method listed first, they are:

- A trusted advisor recommending that a person use the product

- A top rating by an advisory service

- A friend telling a friend (in person, by phone, and increasingly by e-mail)

- People giving you a reference, referral, or otherwise networking

- Expert/peer word-of-mouth sessions—teleconferenced or face to face

Figure 11-1
Relative credibility of word-of-mouth delivery methods

In Marketer's Control

Independent

Both message and media in marketer's control

You completely control messages, and you control, buy, or rent media.

Traditional media:

    Advertising

    Direct mail

    Brochures

Word of mouth simulations

Paid endorsements

Hotlines, call centers

Faxback services

Web pages

Group selling, dinner meetings, etc.

← Salespeople, reps, agents → (varies)

Both the messages and the media through which they flow are independent but influenceable.

Pure word of mouth (friends, colleagues, etc., telling peers)

Spontaneous expert endorsements

Studies, papers, articles by experts

Spontaneous media coverage

Independent rating services, magazine ratings

Independent referrals and networking

E-mail, electronic forums, etc.

← Word-of-mouth incentive programs

Not very credible, when compared to the others (sorry)

Most credible

Decreasing Crediblity

Much less credible

A little less credible

Message only in control

You control message. Media is relatively independent but influenceable.

← PR, publicity: events, placements, promotions, → (varies)

Announcements

Customer service as a word-of-mouth engine

Message is relatively independent (but influencable). You control media.

Live, teleconferenced expert word-of-mouth sessions

Live, teleconferenced peer word-of-mouth sessions

Other company sponsored seminars

Trade show events/opportunities

Advisory groups (customers, suppliers, experts, salespeople)

Expert roundtables (published or taped)

Speakers programs

Networking events

Testimonials

"Canned" word of mouth: videotapes, audiotapes, etc.

- Peer word-of-mouth sessions—teleconferenced or face to face

- Experts' roundtables

- Experts and customers quoted in articles recommending the product (PR)

- Experts' speeches, papers, studies, and other endorsements.

- Videotaped or audiotaped sessions of experts and peers endorsing a product (infomercial style)

- Advisory groups

- User groups—especially electronic forums and teleconferences

- Networking at conferences, association meetings, or seminars

- Product seminars conducted by a nonsalesperson at a company

- Events—such as dinner meetings, swap-meets, barbecues, or rallies—mixing customers and prospects

- Quotes from real customers in print ads, mailings, brochures, or commercials

- Quotes from experts in print ads, mailings, brochures, or commercials

- The company president talking to you in a commercial

- Celebrity endorsements

- Actors portraying customers in ads

- Actors portraying experts (such as doctors) in ads

Word-of-Mouth Checklist

To help determine what are the most effective, simple things that can be done to increase your word of mouth and ultimately increase your sales, ask the following questions:

- ❏ Are all of your communications sending the same, *simple message*? It can't generate and survive word of mouth unless it's simple, and unless it's a compelling story.

- ❏ Is your product *positioned* as part of a *general class*, then *differentiated* on the basis of its most *needed attribute*? That's the way people hold things in their heads: "The dandruff shampoo that doesn't dry your hair," "The cereal that adults have grown to love," "The luxury 4-wheel drive." If you can't state your product in such succinct terms, chances are your customers will not be able to describe your product either. And if your product can't survive word of mouth, it probably can't survive at all.

- ❏ Are your examples *outrageous* enough to be repeated? Is there any earthly reason for people to repeat your story?

- ❏ Do you sprinkle your materials with *success stories* from real people?

- ❏ Are you using *experts* fully, in ways that are objective but effective?

- ❏ Have you created mechanisms so that people can *follow up* on the word of mouth they hear: simple and multiple ways of inquiring, investigating, ordering?

- ❏ Have you made the *decision process*—i.e., the collection of information, confirmation, trial, and rollout—so *easy* that your customer does not have to exert any effort?

- ❏ Have you created events and mechanisms so that once your prospect hears about your product, it is *easier to try or buy* than to stay with the frustration and uncertainty of unful-filled desire?

❏ *Advertising:* Do you have success stories from real people in at least some of your ads? How about quotations from customers and experts? Have you tried giving information that people can rip out and give their friends? How about offering useful booklets or invitations to events such as seminars? There are dozens of ways of increasing word of mouth through advertising if you make it a primary objective, not an afterthought or nonthought!

❏ *Sales:* Have you trained your salespeople in how to get referrals, recommendations, and testimonials? Do you know how to "work the booth" at trade shows? Do you have a program that teaches your salespeople how to master these activities? Do you have a referral system in place—a rewards system for getting and making referrals? Are you making use of the word of mouth among your sales force? What are they telling each other? Are they turning each other on or off? Are you making use of the positive word of mouth of your most successful salespeople in order to motivate your less successful salespeople? Are you taking advantage of the word-of-mouth opportunities at trade shows?

❏ *Direct mail:* Are you asking for referrals from your customers? Have you identified your most enthusiastic customers and offered them special incentives to refer their colleagues? Are you taking advantage of the other opportunities mentioned above, particularly customer stories, case studies, and the like? Are you offering customers something genuinely valuable, such as a useful booklet, and getting their colleagues' names to add to your recipient list?

❏ *Internet:* Are you taking advantage of the myriad opportunities for networking, interactive information, and other word-of-mouth opportunities that this medium—the most important word-of-mouth medium ever invented—offers?

❑ *Service:* Are you viewing customer service—which is much, much broader than fixing broken product—as a branch of marketing, as an opportunity center instead of a cost center? Are you going to extraordinary lengths to satisfy people, so that they will talk about how well you took care of them?

❑ *In general:* Is your entire marketing program oriented toward generating, encouraging, and amplifying every word-of-mouth opportunity possible? It's easy to get people to talk about the outrageous, and it's easy to be responsibly, professionally outrageous.

If you are not yet looking at your entire marketing program from a word-of-mouth perspective, you have a mega-opportunity to impact your sales dramatically, quite possibly to levels that are severalfold beyond their present numbers.

Building a Professional Practice through Word of Mouth

Most of the ideas in this book can be applied directly or adapted to professional practices, but there is natural reluctance for some professionals to apply "commercial" or "product" ideas to their areas. Understandably, professionals are so turned off by "crass commercialism" that it can be difficult to take product ideas and hold them in mind long enough to adapt them to the kind of extremely individual, personalized service inherent in a professional practice. So, let's directly address "building a practice" through word of mouth.

Let's take a very broad definition of professional practice, which includes the following:

- Formal professions, such as physicians, lawyers, psychologists, accountants, or architects

- Consultants in management, marketing, marketing research, finances, or time-management

- Agents, such as real estate agents, literary agents, or theatrical agents

- Tradespeople, such as a plumbers, carpenters, or appliance repairers

- Various other "practices" where an individual or small group gives personalized service of a highly individual and often idiosyncratic nature

These types of businesses are almost totally dependent upon word of mouth, even more than the other businesses mentioned in this book. Why? Because in a practice, your "products" are the *results* you create. And the results you create—your value—are a direct result of your *personal competence*. Your customers, clients, or patients are directly at your mercy. In contrast, the value of most other products is the result of a complex interaction of teams of people designing, manufacturing, delivering, and servicing the product or service. The focus is appropriately on the company, the product, or the service. These products are often more easily evaluated directly because they are known beforehand. They are often standardized and predictable. In a practice, people are buying *you*—your knowledge, experience, competence, ethics, and personality—not some specifically predetermined output, product, or even service. Usually, they are buying your *future ability* to diagnose problems and create solutions.

This is an inherently more uncertain process than with other products. This extreme uncertainty means that prospects and customers need extreme amounts of reassurance and vicarious experience—the kind that conventional marketing cannot deliver. After all, how do you try a surgeon, or a life insurance agent? In the first case, you can't let several surgeons cut "a little bit," and then pick the winner. Or, in the case of life insurance, dying to see if the policy will pay off isn't practical. The only way to try is to try vicariously, through someone else's experience. The sharing of experience—as we've seen earlier—is an often overlooked function of word of mouth.

An additional reason that these practices are so dependent on word of mouth is that it is often prohibitively expensive to advertise, or it's considered unethical (or at least frowned upon), or it's impossible to put into an ad or brochure what you really want to say. Remember, you are selling *you*. How do you say in any credible way that you are the most caring, smartest, most ethical, most responsive, cleverest, most creative, most knowledgeable, and just plain nicest person on the face of the Earth, or at least in your profession? It's pretty hard to do without seeming to boast or seeming to put your competitors down.

So, how do you get to the top of your profession, craft, trade, cottage industry, consultancy, or other heap? You get there by creating what Ken Blanchard calls "raving fans"—in your case, "raving clients." *Satisfied* clients are not enough. They have to be *raving* about you in order to spark a word-of-mouth explosion. How do you create that? The same way as I've advocated in the rest of this book: by being *outrageously outstanding*, and by making sure that people know it and communicate it.

How?

Above all, give people something—preferably outrageously outstanding—to talk about. Identify the one or two areas where you can distinguish yourself, such as service, responsiveness, friendliness, or expertise. Then take these areas several outrageous steps beyond where you are now. If you're the most knowledgeable, write articles, give speeches, and chair committees. If you're the most personable, make videotapes, network, and have phone hours or in-person seminars. Make sure everything you do in your area of distinction is surprisingly beyond expectations.

In case you think you are not able to distinguish yourself, you need to realize that most people—even in the highest-level professions—are satisfied with being merely adequate, despite what they say. If you make yourself one of those very few people who really try to be the best they can be, you will quickly put yourself beyond most of your competitors. And you don't have to be beyond everybody. If some people are raving about you, and other people are raving about someone else, you will *both* have more business than you can handle. All you're trying to do is keep your practice filled easily, at high enough fees so that you can also have the time to enjoy the rest of life.

Here are some specific suggestions and examples, to be modified according to your circumstances, your clients, and most of all your personal style and abilities. For instance, if you speak well but write terribly, stress speaking, get writing coaching, or hire a writer who can pull the info out of you and put it into writing.

First of all, get a copy of Dr. Paddi Lund's *Building the Happiness Centred Business.* Yes, "centred" is spelled right if you live in Australia, which Paddi does. He is a dentist who hated dentistry and his life. He spent all his professional time causing pain and dealing with staff and clients who didn't bring him satisfaction. He was about to go crazy (literally) when he realized that he needed to make some major changes. So he rethought dentistry. I don't want to give away too much of his book (if you are in a professional practice, you *have* to read it), but in summary here's what he did.

He talked to his patients and his staff to find out what they didn't like. Then, he totally rethought all of the assumptions about how a dental practice was supposed to operate. He replaced the reception area and its counter with individual lounge areas where patients could be interviewed by "care nurses," who were totally responsible for all aspects of the care of patients. He actually took a chain saw to the counter one weekend.

He realized that most dental procedures could be accomplished in one several-hour visit instead of several one-hour visits.

So, he takes only one or two patients a day. Instead of taking weeks to work on most people, he takes less than a day!

People told him that the thing that they most hate about dentistry (aside from the pain) is the smell. He experimented with everything he could to mask the smell, and the only thing he found was the smell of fresh baking. So, he hired a baker, who meets people with baked goods that they prefer and offers to bake anything they want, since they'll be there several hours.

He has "fired" all his patients who were headaches, and won't keep an employee who is not having fun. He has a referral-only practice. There is no sign on his door, except one that says that it is a referral-only practice and that someone in need of care who has not been referred will be happily referred to another dentist. He has an unlisted phone number!

He works about 22 hours a week, and makes at least three times more money than his most successful colleagues. People fly to him from all over the world! Read the details in his book. His Web site is www.solutionspress.com.au.

See also Appendix E for an illustration of his book promotion.

Paddi is successful because he is totally focused on his customers', team's, and own happiness. How could people *not* talk about him? How could patients *not* refer people to him? Yet, I've told this story to hundreds of physicians, dentists, and other professional practitioners. Instead of begging me to tell them how to get his book, (It's very hard to get. You can essentially get it by referral only!) and dropping everything to find out more, most of the time their eyes glaze over and they change the subject, or if it's in a speech they start fidgeting and stop taking notes.

I think it's because most people don't have the guts to do the things that will make them stand out. In fact, we say, "stick out like a sore thumb." We don't usually have a positive analogy to denote sticking out (all right, maybe we do, but you get the idea). In our mad rush toward democracy and equality (which has to do with having an equal *vote*, not being the same), we are afraid to stand out above other people in the pursuit of excellence. We all know that if we stand out, many people won't like us.

Read about Paddi Lund, adapt his methods to your situation, and then be prepared for all the grief that happiness brings you.

On a more modest scale, one of the country's leading ophthalmologists, Robert Snyder in Tucson, has been a guest expert on many of our word-of-mouth teleconferences. He has advocated to thousands of other ophthalmologists that they call every surgical patient the evening of their surgery. He does it and reports that patients are bowled over. They are amazed. They never had a doctor call *them* and express concern. He says that it is the best practice builder he has ever discovered. His patients don't care as much about his international reputation as they do about this simple expression of concern. They tell their friends. It takes eight minutes a night, but his practice has a big backlog.

The most amazing thing about it is that Bob tells me that very few ophthalmologists have taken his advice. I don't think it's because they are lazy. I think it's because they just don't want to be outrageous. They don't realize that they can be *constructively* outrageous!

Two other ophthalmologists that I know, Eric Donnenfeld and Henry Perry, also have very successful practices, on Long Island, New York, and have also been part of our faculty in our pharmaceutical teleconferences. They are among the leading experts in corneal and external diseases of the eye. What really impresses their patients is not that they seem to be involved with doing clinical studies of every important development in their areas of ophthalmology (which is true), but that they let their patients watch a live eye operation from the waiting room, and then watch the patient walk out to the waiting room to look out of the window and read a "keep off the grass" sign and a parking sign that he couldn't read before! Think of the effect this has on the patients in the waiting room when they see someone screaming for joy at the new clarity of his eyesight!

These are not "tricks." These are expressions of concern and a desire to spread their standards of excellence and the enthusiasm they have for their work, which comes through in everything they do.

Then, there's Alan Weiss. He is the author of *Million Dollar Consulting, Money Talks: How to Make a Million as a Speaker* and many other popular books. He's an extremely busy consultant and speaker. Yet, he returns phone calls within 90 minutes. (So he says, but he's always returned my calls within 30 minutes!) He gives his clients unlimited access to him, even on weekends. Yet, he manages to live a balanced life, working at his pool, and having plenty of leisure time. How? He realized that people don't waste his time. They have better things to do. He has learned to have efficient conversations. In fact, they don't call him on weekends, even though he has given them permission to call if there is an emergency. (I've always done the same thing, and in 30 years I've had one Sunday call, from a client whose product was going to be attacked on "60 Minutes" that night!) People don't make him travel to their offices more than is reasonable because they can't afford to spend the time. When you call him, you reach him. He does many other surprising things that are too numerous to mention. Read *Million Dollar Consulting* if you are a consultant. I was so impressed that I hired him myself as a consultant. The unusually valuable things he does make people recommend him, as I am doing now.

Always focus on value: What can you give people that will make what you do more beneficial to them? Give seminars. Write useful booklets. Write newspaper articles. Put up a genuinely useful Web site. Give, give, give.

Get continual feedback from your customers on how you are doing. Do surveys, have other people do phone interviews. Ask people how you are doing. People who complain actually care. The others walk. Ask for suggestions. Ruthlessly reexamine all of your assumptions. Why do you do business the way you do? Do you really have to? What if you didn't accept the constraints that you think you have to accept?

For instance, there are a growing number of physicians and psychologists who are opting out of so-called managed care (it's actually "managed cost"). They were forced to practice in a sub-optimum way, dictated by cost considerations. Their professional judgment was co-opted by people whose standard was not *best* care, but *cost-effective* care. Some physicians are accepting a flat rate to take care of people's routine medical needs, charging a fee for additional service. Some are making a little less money, but enjoying their profession more. Others are actually making considerably more money. It doesn't take much to perform the wildly extraordinary service that gets people to talk about you.

You might consider a "referral-only" practice, like Paddi Lund mentioned above. You pretty much have a referral-only practice anyway. Why not weed out the people who don't give you satisfaction and ask the others to refer to you the kind of people for whom you will provide loving care?

I once brought a TV to a repairman who called a day later and told me that the set had miraculously come back to life. He said that he could charge me for a complete diagnosis, but recommended that I pick up the set without charge and try using it until it stopped working again. He said that this could be a day or ten years, so why spend the money? The set is still going strong years later, but I've sent a lot of customers to him. An honest TV repairman? Wow!

Give people genuinely useful materials that they can give their friends. That way, they will communicate with their friends about you while giving their friends something that is genuinely useful.

I once talked with a group of ten patients who had been among the first to get bifocal intraocular lenses implanted. We totaled up the estimated number of people that these folks had talked with. It was over 4000! How? Several of them spoke at various AARP meetings and other clubs and organizations. The particular surgeon whose patients they were (I believe it was in San Diego, but I don't remember his name) did a number of interesting things. He had these patients literally hold the hands of other patients who were undergoing cataract surgery (people are fully conscious during such surgery). The patient assistant was trained to talk the person through what was going on, so that the surgeon could concentrate on his surgery. They also gave presurgery talks and seminars. You bet both the hand-holders and the hand-holdees talked to everyone they could.

Be Outrageous

Are there unconventional ways that you can involve your patients, clients, and customers in your work? Don't be quick to say no. Give it some creative thought.

Above all, do what's constructively outrageous, unexpected, surprising—whatever will make a good story for people to tell. I'm not advocating coming to work as a clown, although come to think of it, it worked for Patch Adams. People's lives are mostly routine. Everyone wants a good story to tell. Give good stories to people, and they'll tell them.

Call someone from a foreign country. Instead of waiting three days to do a five-minute task or follow-up, do it now and blow someone away. Send someone whose business you value a crazy gift. Hold a party for your patients. Give them a free seminar. I once distributed a list of my competitors for the times when I was completely booked up. Funny thing. Almost everybody waited. Those who didn't came back. Give away business and know-how to your "competitors." Not, of course, competitors whom you consider unethical or incompetent. Just competitors who are better than you in some respects, so that everybody wins. It sends the message that you are not afraid for people to find out about your best competitors. Only the best could be that secure, which is exactly what a client said to me! They'll be a source of word of mouth, referring people back to you. I get more business now from people whom I considered competitors 20 years ago than from almost any other source.

My wife is training director at a prestigious New York Gestalt psychotherapy training institute. She gives lectures and demonstrations all over, because her strength is in teaching through demonstration, drawing principles and techniques from experience. Writing is more difficult for her, so she goes with what she is spectacular at, in her own quiet way. She is focused on expanding the skills of therapists. What happens? Therapists come to her for therapy and supervision. They send people to her whom they think they can't handle. They send children and spouses of their patients, whom they may feel they can't see without creating problems with their patients. People bring along friends to her demonstrations. Maybe someday she'll do videotapes, or Web classes or something else. The point here is that you have to put yourself out there, in your style, outrageously but without hype.

Maybe you want to quietly fill a practice, without being obtrusive. Maybe you don't want people to notice you. Maybe you don't want to attract attention. Maybe you think I have some advice for you if you fit this profile. I don't.

There are probably ten things that you can do regularly that suit your style and skills. Send me examples of the ones that worked best at grs@mnav.com and you may see them on our Web site or in the next edition of this book.

The Word-of-Mouth Toolkit

Word of mouth is too important to leave up to your customers! This statement may seem strange, because it is your customers who are the people who transmit word of mouth. However, if you give people something to talk about and motivate them to talk about it, and leave it there, you are missing an important element, and your word-of-mouth campaign is likely to fizzle.

If you leave word of mouth up to your customer, you are assuming that the customer is able to represent your product accurately and in an exciting manner. You are assuming that your customers are able to figure out who should be exposed to your product or service, and that they will be receptive to the messages that excite your present customers. You assume that your customers are able to answer questions that they didn't have when they made their decision. In other words, you are assuming that your customers will be able to do a job that your salespeople can barely do. You are assuming that enthusiasm confers articulateness. It does not.

These—and many other similar assumptions—are just plain wrong. You spent a lot of time and money (at least I hope you did) figuring out just how to describe your product in ways that communicate it accurately, get people excited, and cause them to be persuaded. You have conducted word-of-mouth research (described in Chapter 8) to hear your most persuasive customers convince others. It's only a small handful of your customers who can be this persuasive. (By the way, these are not the customers who sound the best. They are the customers who actually refer the highest number of eventual customers.) Even this handful could be a lot more persuasive if they had a little help. Your *average* customers could be spectacularly more persuasive with a little help, which they would welcome. After all, they want their friends to benefit from your wonderful product and will welcome any reasonable help in bringing the information to the right people, who will then thank them for recommending your product.

The vehicle for this is what my friend, colleague, and former partner Ron Richards calls the Word-of-Mouth Toolkit. Here is the way he describes it:

> Assume that you are a Web site owner who has allies that would like to talk about the site, community, or product, but they are missing a whole bunch of tools. The word-of-mouth tool kit gives them on a silver platter everything they need to be word-of-mouth allies, and removes the need to reinvent the wheel. The non-Internet version is a folder that has booklets, checklists, and worksheets to give your friends. It even has toolkits within the toolkit. For instance, it contains things such as:

- A list of the kinds of people you might want to contact about it. Instead of saying, friends, colleagues, or relatives, say, probably the best people to tell of this are [give criteria for selecting people]. For instance, in the case of a digital camera, you might want to tell your friends, colleagues, and relatives who are interested in digital photography but want ease and simplicity.

- The need they have to have to make them interested.

- The brief description of the product: Why reinvent a description that is clear and compelling? Include a description that people have found makes the product clear.

- Questions and answers (really answers to qualms).

- Dos and don'ts: almost sales training. DON'T use the words "sales training," but assume that people want to persuade their friends, and be open about it.

This approach helps people start successfully. That's very important, because if a person doesn't receive a positive reaction in the first try or two, he or she will turn off and stop trying.

Ron further points out that the Word-of-Mouth Toolkit should contain an additional bonus, aside from the worth of your product. It should contain some news, some new learning, some urgent or critical information that your customers and the people with whom they are talking will find honestly exciting.

Ron and I have both constructed Word-of-Mouth Toolkits that have caused multifold sales increases. Any product that doesn't have this material designed specifically to facilitate customers communicating with their friends or colleagues is operating on a fraction of its marketing power.

Here are some additional ideas:

■ Have a separate path on your Web site for customers to use in order for people to demonstrate your product to their friends. A demo with a friend is radically different from a solo demo. Design it accordingly. For instance, it might have simplified screens, since a knowledgeable user is going to be operating it. Or, it may have prompts such as, "At this point, you might want to ask your friend to show you how he has applied this."

■ Do the same thing with a brochure. A brochure differs from a sales aid, since a sales aid is designed to be presented by a salesperson. Similarly, a word-of-mouth brochure differs from both a sales aid and a brochure. For instance, it has places where your customer can demonstrate or talk about her own experience.

■ Give samples that friends can give to friends.

■ Give special offers that can be honored only through the friend.

■ Make it clear to the person being referred what the referrer is getting. In general, people don't want to make money off of something that a friend does. People tend to say, "if he needed the money, why didn't he ask me?" But if there is a general incentive, such as an improved product due to a larger user base (not true of all products), or greater standardization if one product is accepted, or just helping a deserving product succeed, then it tends to be accepted. Also, it is more persuasive when a friend is making a recommendation without monetary incentive.

■ Give people the ability to access (via Web site, faxback, or any other means) preprinted materials such as e-mails that people can modify themselves to use as a base in communicating. For instance, Microsoft regularly produces PowerPoint™ slide shows so that MIS people can use them to convince their top management to upgrade to a new program or operating system. Knowing that MIS people are not necessarily professional communicators, Microsoft gives them a framework of a presentation, including how to construct a financial analysis of what they are proposing, so that people can have a start.

CHAPTER 12

Practical Tips and Suggestions

The following tips will get you started, and aid you in coming up with new ideas. Each requires a special expertise and skill set. They are listed to give you a vision of what is possible. Again, let me repeat my previous admonitions: Word of mouth is like playing with fissionable materials. Although it is potentially the most powerful and effective thing that you can do, it is also very dangerous: potentially poisonous, explosive, and corrosive. Don't play with it at home. Leave it to the professionals.

Using Experts
Advisory Groups

No matter how much you know your market, things change rapidly. Get industry experts, your best customers, your salespeople, and suppliers into advisory groups to help you stay ahead of the competition. More important, this locks them into your company, demonstrates your commitment to your industry, makes them feel special, and—most important—sets the stage for word of mouth. They become company spokespeople spontaneously. They also reinforce their positive image of your products to each other. They "get on your side."

Advisory groups can consist of any or all of the following:

Experts

Customers

Salespeople

Suppliers

Tips

1. Many companies do this once a year. I strongly recommend doing this face to face once a year, but by telephone conference several times a year. An hour-long conference call every couple of months is not an imposition on people, given that there is no travel involved.

2. Be frank and open. Don't put positive spins on problems. People will be surprisingly understanding of problems and will help you solve them if you let them.

3. Ask participants directly what would turn people like themselves on. You will be pleasantly surprised that many of their most desired changes are things that you thought were insignificant or too easy to do.

Experts' Roundtables

Conduct sessions with experts "on the record." Transcripts, tapes, or quotes from these sessions can be used in future promotions (obviously with their permission).

Expert Selling Groups

Make sure the experts are reassured that they are free to express their opinions freely. They are very careful about their reputations. You must guard the objectivity of the sessions. The trick is to pick products that are superior for the particular applications and people. Then let a third party conduct unbiased sessions.

Using Seminars, Workshops, and Speeches
Speakers Program

Set up a roster of experts and customers who are willing to be paid spokespeople for your products and services.

Seminars

Conduct useful seminars or classes that will get more people into the areas where your products are used. Seminars are particularly useful where your customers need a certain level of education or skills in order to use your product, or use your products more. They are used much in the financial area, such as seminars on investing for retirement or on municipal bonds.

For instance, a magic store might offer classes on how to perform magic tricks. Once hooked, the people become customers for life. Pharmaceutical companies offer classes on how to diagnose and treat an illness for which it has a treatment.

All of these directly stimulate word of mouth.

User Groups

User groups are similar to seminars, but not as formal. They are self-generated by users. Support these people. They are your customers.

Group Selling

Group selling means selling to several people at the same time. The advantage is that the word of mouth in the group itself—that is, the interaction—will get people more deeply committed than they would be individually. They hear questions that they did not think of themselves. This generates a deeper feeling of completeness than they would otherwise feel. Also, they are not "on the spot" in a group, so will feel more comfortable.

Tip: How to sell people in groups to take advantage of word of mouth is a whole new level of skill for your salespeople. Build it into your training program. It can increase the productivity of your sales force multifold.

Dinner Meetings

Invite customers and prospects to a dinner at which a presentation of your product is shown. These meetings are included here for completeness, but in 99 percent plus of all cases teleconferences will be more effective.

Expert and Peer Selling Groups

It is better when the information comes from experts and/or peers. Experts show the upside, while peers show the real-world potential of the product. Each is essential to the decision process.

Teleconferenced Experts' Panels

As mentioned repeatedly in earlier chapters, this is by far the most powerful form of word-of-mouth delivery. Interestingly, when asked whether they would prefer face-to-face sessions, or teleconferenced sessions, most people choose face to face. But when they are given the choice in an actual invitation, most people opt for sessions conducted by telephone conference call.

"Canned" Word of Mouth
Videotapes, Audiotapes, CDs, and Web Sites

You can produce videotapes, audiotapes, CDs, or Web presentations in order to show expert roundtables and individual testimonials. These are used all the time on TV commercials.

Referral Selling
Testimonials

Testimonials, one of the most powerful marketing tools, are *the* way of selling movies and books. They are overlooked in most other fields, or regarded as unprofessional or inappropriate. But there is almost always a way of using testimonials in a powerful way.

People think it's hard to get testimonials and that people will not believe them. Both are very costly beliefs.

To get testimonials, just ask for them! Ask your customers for feedback about your product or service. Whenever people say anything particularly complimentary, ask whether you can quote them. Most people will allow you to quote them.

A CASE IN POINT

Two days after President Nixon announced his wage/price controls, I ran a teleconference of eight of the country's leading economists to predict what would happen. Milton Friedman, the Nobel prize—winning economist, voiced skepticism about whether the conference would be productive, given the informal nature of it and the fact that people would not be face to face. Nevertheless, he was willing to participate, which he did from his vacation home in Vermont. When I called him the next day, he said that it was the most productive roundtable discussion he had ever participated in—much more orderly and informative than if it had been conducted face to face. (Remember, this was in 1972, long before the conference call had been widely accepted.) I reminded him of his previous skepticism, and asked if I could quote him, as a service to other people who might also wonder if such a discussion could be orderly, open, and informative. He enthusiastically agreed, giving me a powerful tool to overcome skepticism among potential participants and clients.

It's that simple: Ask. But ask as a service to other people who might benefit from what you offer, not as a favor to you.

When you ask if you may quote them, send them three quotes. One is an outrageous rave. One is an extremely positive one, and the last one is just positive. Obviously, make them relevant to the persuasion step that you are trying to accomplish. Make it clear that you are doing it for their convenience and out of respect for their time, and obviously they should feel free to make any changes, or to submit a complete rewrite. Make boxes so that they can check and initial the selection they are giving permission for. Often, they will select the one in the middle, which is more than good enough (sometimes the top rave lacks credibility). (I'm indebted to Wendy Keller, my literary agent, for this suggestion and have been using it with great success.)

When using testimonials, make sure you have permission, of course. Use full names and company affiliations if people will permit it. If not, use full names and city. Less effective is using initials, but if that's all you can get, do it. If people won't let you quote them by name, use their quote anyway, without attribution, which can still be extremely powerful.

Networking

Go to every event where you might meet customers and competitors. Yes, competitors. Throughout my career, about 25 to 50 percent of my business has been referred to me by so-called competitors. Others who aren't afraid of competitors tell me the same thing. Join industry associations, attend networking events, talk to competitors (especially ones who have slightly different specialties and who might be referral sources), participate in appropriate electronic forums, speak at meetings, etc. Get out there. Collect cards. Call people. Help people get information. Everything will come back to you in more business and personal satisfaction.

Referral Selling Program
Setting Up a Referral Selling Program

Make sure all your people, particularly salespeople and service people, are trained and get practice in referral selling. Give them incentives for getting referrals. Make sure they are tracked visibly. Make sure you have a mechanism for immediately following up on the referrals.

Referred customers are at least ten times more likely to buy from you than prospects who come from cold calls. A referred prospect *who calls you* as a result of being referred by a friend is about a hundred times more likely to do business with you. Treat them like old friends, and thank and/or reward the referrer.

How to Get Referrals

Basically, you have to ask your enthusiastic customers, "Who should I be talking with about my services? Who would benefit most?" Again, present it as a service to the potential referee, not as a favor the referrer is doing for you. Ask people to pass along your literature. I know, it's obvious, but people just don't do it enough.

In addition, give people incentives for passing along names to you. Give them a free product, or a free month of service. You get the idea.

Give people samples and literature to pass along to their friends.

Look at It as an Entire "Referral Selling System"

You should have a steady stream of prospects coming to you directly from your customers. Customers should also be sending you a steady stream of names of qualified prospects so that you can pursue them. Most companies don't. But if they did, those companies could at least double their sales by building a customer referral system. Isn't that worth some major resources? Isn't that worth a few focus groups of people who referred several other people, to find out what motivated them and what they said and did that was successful? Isn't it worth a few focus groups to talk with people who were actually referred and who followed up and became customers? What motivated *them?* What triggered their initial interest? What barriers did they have to overcome? What clinched the sale?

Write materials specifically designed to stimulate customer referrals. These need to be carefully constructed according to the same rigorously applied persuasion principles as other materials: the right content, from the right people, in the right sequence.

Companies can at least double their sales by building a customer referral system.

Do you have materials designed to help friends refer friends? Different materials for advisors referring less sophisticated clients? Wives to sell husbands? Creative types to sell financial types? You get the idea.

Using the Different Media

Use the "new" media by setting up hotlines, faxback services, Internet-based word of mouth, forums, e-mail, and call centers. All of these can be turned into powerful word-of-mouth generators. But you can also use the traditional media to generate word of mouth.

Customer Service as a Word-of-Mouth Engine

Several books have been written about using customer service to generate word of mouth. FedEx was built on this idea. Once again, read *Positively Outrageous Service*, by T. Scott Gross.

PR: Placements, Events, and Promotions

If you don't have an aggressive PR program in place, put it in place. Remember that PR is not just about getting your name in publications. Hold word-of-mouth generating events and promotions.

Ads, Sales Brochures, and Direct Mail

Again, how many times have you seen people who are obviously actors playing the part of real customers, when real customers would be much better? Put your customers in your ads, brochures, and direct mail pieces. Have them tell their stories.

Salespeople

Word of mouth among your salespeople can make or break your product. Salesperson programs, sales stars, and peer training can all be used to help generate word of mouth. Our company does a lot of word-of-mouth research among salespeople, and there is no question that if the salespeople aren't sold, your product doesn't stand a chance. They have their own grapevine. You can get the best salespeople to teach the other salespeople how to better sell your product. Get the success stories of the salespeople and the customers transmitted to all the salespeople.

How to Spur the Stampede

We have now come full circle. We have examined word of mouth in more detail than it has ever been scrutinized before. We have examined why it is effective, how to research it, and how to organize a word-of-mouth campaign and how to deliver it.

Now what?

I would like to respectfully suggest that you get serious about word of mouth. Put someone in charge and let him or her build a team. Treat word of mouth as a separate discipline. If you are really serious, that person should be a vice president on the level of your vice presidents of advertising or marketing, whose mission is to change your marketing from a mass marketing and broadcast paradigm to a word-of-mouth paradigm. That person should be empowered to cross the lines of all marketing functions, plus service, sales, product development, and any other function that impacts what people are saying about your products and your company. In any conflicts between the other functions, it is the potential for positive word of mouth that should drive what you do, since it's word of mouth that triggers trial, sales, continued usage, and expanded usage, in other words, action.

That being said, who do you go to in order to construct word-of-mouth campaigns? Advertising agencies tend to understand mass media, not interactive one-on-one marketing. PR agencies tend to understand how to get stories inserted into media, but most lack the specialized understanding needed for other kinds of word-of-mouth events. Educational companies tend to be able to put together seminars and conferences, but with little understanding of and regard for the subtleties of word-of-mouth marketing. Seminars have to be built from a deep understanding of word-of-mouth needs, not only from what would be interesting educationally. Word-of-mouth marketing is a separate discipline that involves working with live, highly influential, people.

There is a need for word-of-mouth agencies or consultancies that construct word-of-mouth campaigns. As I said in the Introduction, a whole new set of agencies is going to spring up, populated by people who understand interactive marketing, and who understand the dynamics of word of mouth.

If you discover any such agencies, please let me know about them and I'll post them on our Web site.

CHAPTER 13

The Secrets of Word-of-Mouth Marketing

These secrets of word-of-mouth marketing are principles that are generally unknown, unaccepted, forgotten, or ignored among the marketing community. They are probably not acted upon by your competition, and therefore they will provide you with a tremendous competitive edge.

Even if any of these ideas contradict your belief system, why not try them and see where they lead you. Look at them from this new perspective. You can always reject them later, but don't reject them too soon.

The first two sections are secrets of marketing and secrets of decision acceleration that you need to understand in order for the secrets of word of mouth to be used most effectively. Consider them a bonus.

Five Secrets of Marketing

Secret #1: Contrary to popular opinion, marketing is one of the noblest of all professions.

Don't accept—on any level—the idea that marketing is inherently sleazy.

Do realize that you are bringing customers products and services that enhance their lives and make their lives easier.

Do keep at the forefront of your mind the value that your product is specifically providing to the customer. It is the enthusiasm that comes from the value of your product that will help you come up with the reasons people should talk about it.

Do continually remind yourself that the customer is lucky to have your product, that you are providing value, that you are doing the customer a favor by selling your product, just as much as the customer is doing *himself* (not you) a favor by buying it.

Do think about what is so interesting about your product that people would actually want to talk about it with other people. Make sure that you have plenty of these word-of-mouth stimulators.

Secret #2: Marketing is not something that you do to your target (the customer), it is a service for the customer.

Don't approach marketing as something you do *to* the customer. It is something you do *for* the customer.

Don't think in terms of "targets and hits." This leads to battering, intrusive, loud campaigns that just raise the level of noise one or two notches and are largely ignored.

Do realize that marketing isn't selling product(s). *It's getting and keeping customers through providing the service of helping your customer to buy your products.*

Do make customers decide to buy your product by making your product the easy and simple choice.

Don't emphasize self-serving features; instead, emphasize genuine benefits that really make a difference—benefits that people will talk about.

Do make a sale, not a sales pitch. Better yet, make a relationship.

Secret #3: Helping your customer to make the best decision means that you have to have the best product for that customer.

Do get into emotional touch with what is so great about your product. Your customer has to feel desire in order to talk with others and to buy. If you don't feel enthusiasm, you will not spark desire and enthusiasm. People primarily talk with others about things with which they have some sort of emotional involvement.

Secret #4: Honest marketing is not only possible, it is the only sustainable way to gain market advantage.

Do dramatize, dimensionalize, and emphasize the real advantages of your product in the most outrageous—but honest—way. ("Free phone calls on Friday" [Sprint] will get much more word of mouth than "20 percent cheaper.")

Don't tolerate an inferior—or even a "me too" parity—product. Augment it so that it has a clear-cut advantage for the largest number of people.

Don't ever "shade the truth" about anything, anytime, anywhere—especially about your product. When you lie about your product—even by a little shading—you get into the world of fiction. Your mind starts to make up things, rather than sticking with the facts. Your product must work as claimed—or better than claimed—in the real world for a word-of-mouth chain reaction to be sustained.

Secret #5: Believe it or not, the right people actually want to buy your product.

Don't come from trying to convince people. They will resist.

Do come from offering a precious opportunity. If you have to do mental flip-flops to do this, you probably have to do some work on your product and your offering.

Do realize that if people really want the benefit your product offers, all you have to do is help them see it.

Five Secrets of Decision Acceleration

Secret #1: The "best" product doesn't always win. The product that is easiest to decide on wins.

Do realize that in most cases, the best product is the one for which the decision is easiest.

Don't get caught with the "best" product that has a difficult decision cycle. Decision obstacles drop it way down from the top of the list.

Don't sell the customer. Help him buy. Helping the customer buy is helping the customer make the best, easiest, and least time-consuming decision.

Do make your product the easiest product to buy. Root out all obstacles. Ruthlessly go through the decision process and make sure that every bottleneck is eliminated.

Do realize that the most effective thing that a marketer can do is to make the decision easier, and thereby faster.

Secret #2: Decision speed will make or break your product.

Do treat decision speed as the single most important variable in marketing, in most cases more important than brand choice.

Do accumulate customers faster than your competition by making the decision easier than your competition.

Secret #3: The five key stages that people go through in making decisions are the same for everyone. The specifics are all different and will either make or break your product.

Do optimize and accelerate the decision for the customer.

Do thoroughly understand the stages that people go through in making decisions. This is of vital importance because of the next secret. The five stages are:

1. Deciding to decide

2. Selecting among options

3. Trial

4. Implementing/ongoing usage

5. Expanding commitment

Secret #4: There are many secret methods for speeding up the decision process.

Do use unconventional methods, such as outrageous guarantees, giving the product away to get the back-end business, co-marketing, wild offers, outrageous trials, demos, and product challenges.

Do spend as much time focusing on making the decision easier and faster as you spend on getting the customer to chose your product over the competition.

Don't push the customer to go faster. She'll only push back.

Do enable, don't push.

Secret #5: The best way to speed up the decision process is systematically to map out its steps, then remove the bottlenecks.

Do map out how the five stages of the decision cycle apply to your product.

Do ruthlessly go through the decision steps and eliminate all of the hidden obstacles, bottlenecks, and restrictions.

Do make it easier to buy your product than not buy it.

Do understand the differences in decision making for the different types of prospects and customers.

Twenty-Eight Secrets of Word-of-Mouth Marketing

Secret #1: Selling is mostly an illusion.

Do understand that advertisements, salespeople, brochures, and direct mail very rarely sell products *directly*. They almost always work through an intermediate mechanism called personal influence or word of mouth.

Do use word of mouth to multiply the effects of advertising and salespeople.

Don't ever take an ad, send out a mailing, or call on a customer without thinking out the word-of-mouth implications of what you are doing, particularly how to use that vehicle to start, sustain, or intensify a word-of-mouth chain.

Do evaluate every element of marketing by its potential to cause a positive word-of-mouth chain reaction.

Do realize that conventional marketing can—at best—get people interested in your product. Then they talk it over with colleagues, friends, and trusted advisors. It's this word of mouth that triggers their purchase. If they're already interested, your spending more money on conventional marketing is mostly a waste. Spend your money instead on triggering word of mouth.

Secret #2: By influencing word of mouth directly, sales can routinely be increased three to ten times or more!

Don't think small. A new sales campaign or advertising campaign can usually increase sales 10 to 20 percent at most, if it's a smashing success.

Do think big. Shoot for tenfold increases through word of mouth. That way, if you "fail" and only increase sales fivefold, you will still be a hero.

Secret #3: The single most effective method for speeding up the decision process is word of mouth.

Do predigest the decision by showing the customer how someone else made the decision.

Don't look at word of mouth as the way to get people to choose your product.

Do look at it as the way to get people to speed up their decision.

Secret #4: Word of mouth is as easy to structure and use as traditional advertising.

Don't treat word of mouth as just a fortuitous side-effect of your marketing efforts.

Do treat word of mouth as the keystone of marketing, upon which everything else rests.

Do map out a word-of-mouth plan with as much rigor as you plan your advertising, sales campaign, and other aspects of your marketing.

Secret #5: Word of mouth is literally thousands of times as powerful as conventional marketing.

Don't underestimate the power of word of mouth. Everyone

thinks it's important, yet almost everyone seriously underestimates its power. It is at least 1000 times as powerful as conventional marketing.

Don't forget that people act on only a tiny, tiny handful of the thousands of ads, commercials, and sales calls they receive each week. But they act on many, if not most, of the recommendations from friends and trusted advisors.

Do treat word of mouth with the respect—even awe—that it deserves. Your product's reputation is what really sells it: not what you say about it, but what your customers say about it.

Secret #6: Word of mouth is paradoxically the most powerful and most neglected force in marketing.

Do realize that when you neglect something powerful, you are in extreme danger.

Do realize that when you tame something powerful and neglected, you have a powerful secret advantage.

Secret #7: It is almost impossible for your product to succeed unless it has massive positive word of mouth.

Do research the word of mouth that is going on at all levels for your product. Know what people are asking each other and how people are answering.

Do everything you can that is legal and moral to stimulate massive positive word of mouth for your product. That's your first priority as a marketer. Everything else is small potatoes.

Secret #8: Word of mouth either explodes at an exponential rate or it fizzles. There are some specific things that determine what it will be in any case.

Don't use halfway measures to stimulate word of mouth.

Do make it a blitz.

Do plan out your campaign, then throw everything at it that you can—as much as you can, as fast as you can. Word of mouth is a critical mass phenomenon, like nuclear fission. There is no such thing as a gradual, controlled word-of-mouth reaction that has much impact. Go for broke.

Secret #9: There are over a dozen reasons why word of mouth is so powerful. All of these reasons, once understood, can be turned to your advantage.

Do understand exactly from where word of mouth draws its power. That will allow you to exploit its advantages.

Don't assume that word of mouth is powerful only because it's less biased and therefore more credible than advertising. That's only the tip of the iceberg.

Secret #10: There is one overriding characteristic of word of mouth—not its obvious independence and credibility— that gives word of mouth most of its power: Word of mouth is an experience delivery mechanism.

Do realize that the inordinate time it takes to gather experience before, during, and after trial is what holds back products.

Don't push people to get experience (in other words, to try your product).

Do invite them to hear about others' experience.

Secret #11: There are many different types of word of mouth, all potentially controllable.

Don't assume that word of mouth is one global thing: customers talking to prospects.

Do take into account the multiple forms of word of mouth,

such as experts' word of mouth, peer word of mouth, word of mouth among salespeople and dealers, word of mouth among employees, PR, implied word of mouth, endorsements, testimonials, and co-ventures.

Secret #12: Different types of decision makers need different types of word of mouth at each stage of the decision cycle.

Do realize that the key to stimulating the right kind of word of mouth is to realize that there is a right kind of word of mouth for each customer. For instance, innovators don't want to hear "It's tried and true." The early majority aren't impressed with how innovative it is. Each type of adopter needs to hear different things from experts and peers at each different stage of the decision process.

Do identify the exact wording of the word of mouth that will be most successful for each of your different types of customers, particularly the content that will get people past the bottlenecks.

Secret #13: As important as the content is, the sequence and source of the word of mouth is just as important, and sometimes even more important than the content.

Don't try merely to get "positive word of mouth."

Do be precise about the right messages, timing, sequence, and sources of word of mouth. Without all four your word-of-mouth campaign will fizzle.

Secret #14: There are basically two levels of word of mouth, expert and peer word of mouth. Each is more powerful than the other at different stages of the decision cycle.

Don't underestimate the power of experts. One expert endorsement, delivered at the right time, in the right way, from the right person, can result in more sales than your entire sales force can deliver in a year. It only takes a pebble to start an avalanche.

Do use experts to show the upside "ideal" potential of the product.

Don't try to use experts to show how the product will work in the hands of the average user.

Do use peers to show how it works in the hands of the "average Joe or Jane."

Secret #15: In word-of-mouth marketing, confirmation and verification are more important than information.

Don't rely on word of mouth to present the best picture of the product. That's the job of conventional, traditional advocacy media, such as brochures, advertising, and salespeople.

Do use word of mouth to present confirmation and verification of the information. First, people want information, promises, and claims to see what the upside is. Then, if the product promises to make a valuable difference in their lives, they seek confirmation and verification that the claims are really true (verification) and that the product will actually work out in situations similar to their own (confirmation). Verification and confirmation are not sought through conventional marketing channels. They are sought almost entirely through word of mouth.

Secret #16: In word-of-mouth marketing, you are navigating spheres of influence.

Don't approach experts as if they are homogeneous.

Do realize that experts operate from varying spheres of influence. Some are local, others regional, others national or worldwide. Often, the national experts influence the regional and local experts, who confirm each other's opinions when they talk with each other, which results in more firmly held beliefs.

Secret #17: Experts are more approachable than ordinary people, but only through total honesty.

Do use experts. They are much more approachable than you think. But you better be honest and have the better product. You can reach almost anyone if you have a good enough reason.

Do realize that while you think of yourself as having a product, the experts think of your product as a tool. If it is a worthwhile tool, it will solve problems of their constituency (their sphere of influence). That makes them look good, and further reinforces people's image of them as experts. And that makes them want to get behind your product.

Don't try to manipulate experts. They can see it coming miles away. Be open and straight with them. They know exactly where you are coming from and want the best products to succeed.

Secret #18: Credibility is more important in an expert than fame.

Don't confuse expertise with fame. Many experts are unknown. An expert is someone who has vast knowledge, extraordinary thinking ability, and who can apply the knowledge and thinking in the practical world. People almost instantly recognize experts in their field. They attain high credibility when it becomes apparent that they are not only experts, but they are also unbiased, which means that they openly talk about the negatives as well as the positives of your product.

Do choose experts for their credibility, not their fame. Of course, having both is better.

Do realize that experts can be your strongest allies, your most damaging enemies, or totally irrelevant. There are ways to influence each.

Secret #19: There are many reliable mechanisms for delivering word of mouth.

Don't wait for "good word of mouth" as a result of good advertising. You have to make it happen.

Do use workshops, seminars, videotapes, audiotapes, co-ventures, endorsements, testimonials, referrals, networking, PR, the Internet, studies, and all of the other means to deliver word of mouth that are at your disposal.

Do realize that each word-of-mouth delivery channel has its own special set of rules.

Secret #20: Word of mouth must be approached systematically, as a campaign.

Do coordinate, integrate, and systematize your word-of-mouth efforts. Uncoordinated and isolated word-of-mouth events have almost no effect.

Secret #21: The word of mouth among your sales force can be more important than the word of mouth among your customers.

Do sell your sales force first. If they are not sold, who will be?

Don't think that a rah-rah sales meeting will do it. Salespeople, just like other customers, need to see the product accepted by people outside the company before they get fired up.

Do realize that word of mouth is not influenced by management pronouncements. The one thing that overrides everything else in determining the word of mouth among your salespeople, other employees, representatives, dealers, and agents is independent proof that the product is superior.

Secret #22: There is a specific way to research the naturally occurring word of mouth so that you can identify exactly what your customers are actually saying about you, determine what your prospects ask, and conclude whether what your customers say is persuasive.

Don't run conventional focus groups—or worse yet surveys—in which people are asked, "How would you describe the product to a friend?" People don't know, and besides, you need to know the questions that the friend is asking and how the friend is reacting.

Do run unconventional focus groups in which you mix customers and prospects and hear the actual word of mouth.

Secret #23: There is a way to experiment with ways to influence the natural word of mouth and verify that it is in fact persuasive.

Do add to the above-described groups the element of persuasion. Then you can actually hear what changes people's minds.

Secret #24: There are many ways of producing and delivering "canned" word of mouth that are almost as powerful as live, spontaneous word of mouth.

Do "can" word of mouth when you can't deliver it live. Use videotapes, audiotapes, the Internet, transcripts, or magazine reprints. It may seem hokey to you, but this is exactly what your customers want in order to make their decision.

Secret #25: Paradoxically, in word of mouth, unlike in conventional marketing, negatives can be more reassuring than positives about the product.

Don't shy away from letting the negatives into your word-of-mouth communications. In fact, if they are missing, the omission will be glaring and destroy the credibility of whatever material you are presenting. It will make your product "too good to be true." For instance, if you are describing a new piece of software in only glowing terms, people would wait until they had the opportunity to find out what the downside is. By giving them the downside, you actually shorten the decision cycle. This is also particularly true of new drugs: Every drug has side effects. Every physician knows that. Unless there is serious discussion of the side effects, physicians will hold back until they hear about the kind of side effects that people are experiencing in the real world. By talking about the incidence and severity of the side effects, physicians are paradoxically reassured.

Do actually emphasize the negatives, but make sure they are closely followed by ways to cope with the negatives. Everyone expects negatives.

Do realize that people are interested in your product, and want it to work. Often, they will not try it until they feel satisfied that they have a good handle on the negatives.

Secret #26: "Word-of-mouth advertising" is a contradiction in terms.

Don't use the phrase "word-of-mouth advertising." Advertising is advocacy by the company and rarely ever presents a fair picture of the product. It is the exact opposite of word of mouth.

Secret #27: In word-of-mouth marketing, any perceived attempt

to influence the content will totally invalidate the communication.

Don't do anything that will look like you are influencing the content. In fact, if you have the superior product, you won't have to influence the content, just structure it and work with the experts to properly sequence and present their material.

Secret #28: The usual rules of advertising and salesmanship are often counterproductive in word-of-mouth marketing.

Do realize that word of mouth operates by a completely different set of rules from advertising and sales. Word of mouth is a "live" medium. The conventional wisdom of emphasizing the positive, going for the close, dramatizing (or hyping) the benefits, advocacy language, and dozens more just don't apply to word of mouth. They will in fact destroy it.

Don't turn your word of mouth over to your present agencies unless they have demonstrated skills and experience in this area. Word-of-mouth marketing requires special skills that are usually not found in advertising, sales training, promotion, and PR agencies.

CHAPTER 14

An Allegory: The Emperor's New Marketing

Once upon a time not long ago, in a land not far away, there lived an emperor who wanted to promote his kingdom. After all, it had the best scenery, the best doctors, the best workers, the best natural resources, the best companies, and, yes, even the best marketing consultants. But, alas, his in-kingdom advertising wasn't too hot.

He called in ad agencies from far and wide, the best hypemeisters he could find. They all had slick pitches. He picked the agency with the most creative awards, the most appealing ads (the ones the Empress liked best), and the fanciest offices. The hypemeisters told him they would weave him the most creative marketing campaign a kingdom has ever seen.

They put on a big show, with focus groups, surveys, storyboards, and animatics. The campaign was finally ready and was paraded through the land, with great fanfare. The hypemeisters said that only the intelligent and creative could see its true genius. The ads, brochures, sales aids, and Web site were truly something to behold, with gorgeous double-page pictures of natural scenery, beautiful skylines, smiling children, industrial plants, and bustling thoroughfares, printed on silver paper or spectacularly animated with Javascripts.

They all had catchy slogans, clever lines, and zippy copy.

Everyone wondered whether all this glitz would really influence people, but, wanting to be thought creative, they said they loved the campaign, because it was, after all, enormously entertaining. The hypemeisters were overjoyed, thinking of many insertions, hits, and awards.

Until a little boy stepped forward. Being ten years old, he already had so much creativity that he had nothing to prove. He said, "The Emperor's new marketing is naked. It doesn't make any sense. It's pretty, but what does it mean? It's clever, but who cares? It's zippy, but what does it say about what we stand for? It doesn't help anyone make a decision to visit our kingdom, or relocate their factories, or use our products any more than those of any other kingdom. Worse yet, it doesn't make people talk about it. It's woven out of whole cloth so loose that you can see right through it! *The Emperor's marketing has no close!*"

Everyone saw in a flash that the Emperor's new marketing was so full of holes that it might as well not be there. In fact, they found that plain reminder advertising did as well as the fancy glitz.

So they tried a better approach.

- First, they interviewed their customers (evangelists and regular, high and low users), prospects, nonbuying inquirers, rejecters, former users, and nonusers.

- They talked with their sales stars.

- They used special techniques to get beyond the superficial and predictable: For instance, they mixed their evangelists with their interested prospects to hear what actually changed minds through word of mouth.

- They built this proven word of mouth into their marketing mix through testimonials, referral programs, FAQs, and a dozen more methods.

- They mapped out the decision steps needed to adopt the product, and figured out exactly how to help the prospect easily move along the steps.

- They identified the compelling case for several different types of prospects, and they developed interesting materials, seminars, demos, and other materials to present and support the case.

- They validated everything by trying it out with real people, in real situations, to see if it was persuasive and generated increased word of mouth.

- They made it easy and interesting for the prospect to engage in decision making. They made the gathering of information easy and fun, and the trial convenient and conclusive. The customers were supported all the way, instead of badgered.

- They made it easy for their evangelists to evangelize. They gave them tools to invite their friends to experience as well the advantages they had to offer. They made sure these tools survived photocopying, e-mailing, and other means that friends might use to communicate.

All the materials worked together with great synergy as a persuasion system, primarily driven by word of mouth.

People who had *never heard* of the product became interested *prospects*. *Prospects* became *triers*. *Triers* became *adopters* with such a depth of knowledge about what they were doing that the competition didn't have a chance of undoing the decision. And *adopters* became *evangelists*, all but shouting the benefits of the kingdom from the rooftops.

It was simple, well-crafted, customer-empathic marketing. It wasn't particularly clever, although it was very creative in a nonsplashy way. It didn't win any awards. It was hardly noticed, except by prospects and customers. What was noticed was the sales curve. Everyone—the Emperor, the manufacturers, and especially the customers—lived happily ever after. Oh, even the hypemeisters. They went on to another kingdom to do their shtick all over again, but never, ever showed their work to ten-year-old children.

Other Questions That Could Be Asked

Author James Thurber once said, "It's more important to know some of the questions than all of the answers." In the spirit of that quote, you might want to consider the following questions:

- Have our hypemeisters been sitting around talking to themselves, brainstorming when they should be deeply analyzing what's in the minds and hearts of customers?

- Do neon diagrams really sell products, or even attract attention? Do our animated GIFs add or distract?

- Does recall guarantee product success or can people recall ads and still not buy? Or, do they buy without recalling the ads?

- Do our pretty, clever, award-winning materials actually influence decisions?

- How are you going to measure which elements are cost-effective and which are not?

- What are we doing to harness word of mouth, the most powerful force in the marketplace?

- How do we know that our salespeople are really influencing people, or are the sales being made despite the salespeople?

- Has any one of our hypemeisters actually gone out and faced real prospects and turned them around, or even heard it done in a sales call or in a focus group situation?

- Have we actually looked at how people make purchase decisions, and incorporated the latest that is known in the psychology of persuasion?

- Are all these ads, mailings, sales calls, and symposia integrated into a persuasion plan, so that all elements work together, creating synergy, each amplifying each other?

- Have we really gotten inside the heads of our customers, prospects, rejecters, and ex-customers?

- Do we really know why our customers bought, or are we operating on our guesses or their rationalizations? ("I really buy Playboy for the articles, a Mercedes for the engineering, a Gucci bag for its workmanship.")

- Have we uncovered and mapped out their needs, values, wishes, desires, and dreams as well as their conscious and unconscious concerns, qualms, fears, and anxieties?

- Have we targeted our prospects?

- Have we figured out with which prospects we have a chance, and whom we will be wasting our money on?

- Are our products truly positioned, or just tagged with clever slogans?

- Have we identified the actual arguments, the truly compelling case or cases that will actually get people to use our products?

- Do we know the sequence of information that people need, or are we underwhelming them with too little information or overwhelming them with too much?

- Are we covering the different channels that prospects need to get their information?

- Have we taken out the hidden negative language?

- Have we identified the grabbers, hot buttons, and exciting words and concepts that actually turn people on, or just the ones that turn us on?

- Have we actually identified what keeps a customer?

- Have we listened to the word of mouth about us?

- Have we figured out how to turn it to our maximum advantage?

- Most of all, do we have an integrated persuasion strategy and a persuasion system of validated elements all working together?

- Or, do we have a hodgepodge of marketing elements that all try, with varying success, to get across points that *we* think should be made?

- How are the elements supporting each other?

- How are they related to each other?

- Are we making a compelling case, or a series of points?

- In those campaigns that are already implemented, are we getting the results we could be getting?

- If not, why don't we change the approach to one that is customer empathic, one which comes from sound, customer-oriented, persuasion principles, following the decision flow of the customer, instead of product-oriented hype?

CHAPTER 15

The Future

I see a future in which marketing is customer driven. Instead of being passive recipients of "hits" from mass media, customers will determine what they will be exposed to, in what form, in what sequence, and from what sources. They will increasingly turn to the various forms of word of mouth.

This is already happening on the Internet. People go to Web sites in which they are interested, and get information in the sequence that they prefer by choosing which links to click on. They will increasingly participate in forums, e-mail their friends and colleagues, and participate in teleconferenced discussions and in experts' seminars and workshops.

Soon, everyone will be buying products in these radically different ways.

A hundred years ago word of mouth took place either in person, or via handwritten letters. The telegraph, typewriter, telephone, radio, TV, and airmail tremendously increased the ability of people to communicate with each other and to engage in word of mouth. We have now reached another level with e-mail, fax, cell phones, the World Wide Web, list groups, and audio and video teleconferencing. Soon, universal broadband wireless will take us to the next level.

The ability of computers to offer one-to-one marketing (see *The One to One Future*, by Peppers and Rogers), means that word of mouth will be increasingly able to be controlled. People will be able to be selected—and self select—for word-of-mouth sessions, such as seminars, conferences, and referrals.

People can now interact in many different ways with from dozens to hundreds of people who use a particular product. Companies can now conduct product seminars using people regardless of where they are in the world.

E-mail is in some ways the ultimate word-of-mouth medium. For instance, someone may hear about or try a great new product and send a regular e-mail to friends (dozens to thousands). They relay the message to their friends, and so on. The e-mail messages may contain a Web site reference (URL). People can click on the reference and go to the Web site instantly, anywhere in the world.

Listgroups (where dozens to thousands of people all exchange comments via e-mail automatically to everyone in the group) are also a powerful word-of-mouth environment. A limitation of listgroups is that the mailings are limited to the closed interest group who subscribed. It doesn't take advantage of the "friends tell friends who tell friends" potential.

By the time you read this, you'll be able to see TechFrog's site that expands the process beyond a fixed group. Its site enables anyone to e-mail to 10 or 100, who then forward to 10 or 100, etc, etc.—creating for the first time a chain reaction that can grow exponentially, bounded only by the limits of the total Internet population. It's easy and fast for users, and it's free. It's nothing short of providing viral marketing for any person or site that wants it.

The architect of the TechFrogs' viral marketing idea is the colleague who developed many of the word-of-mouth techniques with me, Ron Richards, now President of ResultsLab in San Francisco. The TechFrogs' viral marketing site is full of innovations that Ron hopes will make it the fastest growing viral process in history, and I've learned to take Ron's predictions seriously; he's usually right. You can see it at http://www.techfrogs.com/viralmarketing.

People can, and do, e-mail their friends or colleagues to meet them on an audio conference. As bandwidth increases, multipoint videoconferencing will be as easy as, or even easier than, a regular phone call.

Our means of communication have changed profoundly over the last several decades, and are continuing to evolve at an accelerated pace. And yet, we are almost certainly only at the *beginning* of the Communications Revolution! Yet, marketers are still using decades-old approaches. Sure, everybody's got a Web site. But most are really just online brochures. Media are beginning to blossom into new forms, but fundamental sales communications are the same.

Future marketers will understand the different kinds of people who are their prospects, and they will be able to analyze their decision-making needs. They will offer custom-made, customer-driven information, directly through word of mouth or by using what they learned from word of mouth in other marketing media. They will make the decision easy for the customer. Even though the information gathering is customer driven, it is virtually effortless. When you make it easier for your customer to decide and act than your competitors, the customer tends to go with your product. This accelerates the decision process for your product, allowing you to capture more of the market faster and dominate your market.

Word of mouth, properly delivered, is the easiest way to gather information, and also the most fun. It can, therefore, accelerate positive decisions toward your product and make your sales go through the roof.

What are you waiting for?

Recommended Reading

There are thousands of books on general marketing, thousands on personal selling, thousands on advertising, and hundreds on PR. There are only a handful of books on word of mouth, which is more powerful than all media put together! Word of mouth is so powerful that anything you learn about it that works for you can multiply your sales. On those grounds alone, you should read every book available on word-of-mouth marketing. There aren't that many. There will be more. I'll post them on our Web site, www.mnav.com, where you will be able to purchase them. I applaud these people who have "beaten me to the punch" and hope that all of our work complements each other.

**Michael E. Cafferky, *Let Your Customers Do the Talking*
Chicago, Upstart Publishing, Division of Dearborn
Publishing Group, Inc., 1996**
Subtitled *301+ Word-of-Mouth Marketing Tactics*, it is almost entirely on the tactical level, based on an overwhelming number of ways to get people to talk about you. The author says explicitly that "scientists" do not know why word of mouth works. "It just does." I hope that you have learned in this book why it does. Otherwise, it is a great shopping-list of useful methods to complement the more systematic approach that I have taken. Recommended.

Jerry R. Wilson, *Word-of-Mouth Marketing*
New York, Wiley, 1991

This is an excellent book. It is much more strategic than Cafferky's and nicely complements both my book and Cafferky's. However, it is also centered only on methods for getting people to talk about you and methods of getting publicity. There is little focus on identifying exactly what word of mouth is needed to blast through the bottlenecks, and on ways of delivering word of mouth, other than publicity-generating methods. It does not focus on the different kinds of word of mouth needed for different types of people in different stages of the decision process. It does not mention the Internet, the most important word-of-mouth delivery mechanism in history. It does not mention customer seminars and other events that directly put customer enthusiasts together with skeptics.

Ivan R. Misner, *The World's Best Known Marketing Secret: Building Your Business with Word-of-Mouth Marketing,* **2/e**
Bard Press, 1999

This book is mostly about networking and referral selling, a small part of word of mouth. It mostly talks about building networking organizations.

Godfrey Harris, *Don't Take Our Word for It! : Everything You Need to Know about Making Word-of-Mouth Advertising Work for You*
Americas Group, 1998

Aside from the fact that I object to the term *word-of-mouth advertising* (it's a contradiction in terms), this book is filled with excellent suggestions. There are many new ideas. You would have to be unconscious to not be able to find several things that will dramatically boost your sales.

Everett M. Rogers, *Diffusion of Innovations,* **4/e**
Free Press,1995

I cannot recommend this book more highly. It is must reading for anybody interested in word of mouth. Everett Rogers is a sociologist who has done the definitive work on word of mouth, and his book summarizes thousands of studies and draws principles from them. Reading his first edition decades ago set me on the road to applying what has been learned in a major branch of sociology, called *diffusion theory*, which is almost totally neglected by marketers, but which should be required reading. I only hope that I have added a few new ideas, and added to the practical application of Dr. Rogers' ideas. Brilliant! Bravo!

Elihu Katz and Paul Lazarsfeld, *Personal Influence: The Part Played by People in the Flow of Mass Communications*
Free Press (currently out of print)
This is another must-read classic. And just because it's out of print doesn't mean it can't be found. Inquire on the Internet, or try bookstores that carry used books.

As I predicted, the deluge has begun. The following books have been published in the short span of time it took for this book to go from manuscript to print. Each of these books is doing very well in the business market.

Malcolm Gladwell, *The Tipping Point: How Little Things Can Make a Big Difference*
Little Brown, 2000
A wonderfully readable book that shows that nothing may seem to be going on with a product or idea, but then everything "tips" and everybody suddenly is talking about it. However, Gladwell woefully underestimates the mathematics of how fast word of mouth can spread—orders of magnitude faster than disease contagion.

Seth Godin, *Unleashing the Ideavirus*
Do You Zoom, Inc., 2000
Brilliant, as is everything Godin does. He seems to be the only person who really understands low-friction marketing. What I call

experts, leveraged influencers, and opinion leaders, Godin labels "sneezers." His marketing has been as interesting as the book. He has given away for free about 250,000 books from his Web site, with an estimated passalong rate of four times. That's 1,000,000 free books. Then he self-published at a high price ($40). His first printing of about 25,000 sold out! Highly recommended.

Emanuel Rosen, *Anatomy of Buzz: How to Create Word-of-Mouth Marketing*
Doubleday, 2000
The most rigorously documented of any book on word-of-mouth marketing. Many of the examples that I mention (plus many more), he has documented extensively, so it serves as a wonderful complementary book to this one. *Anatomy of Buzz* is not only very strong on examples, it is also strong on how to implement a word-of-mouth campaign. Rosen's term for my leveraged influencers and Godin's sneezers is "network hubs," and he analyzes their characteristics extensively. Highly recommended.

One last remark: There is a remarkable degree of unanimity among word-of-mouth authors. Some define word of mouth more narrowly, some more broadly, but all are agreed on the basic points about the power of word of mouth, the need to reach influencers, and most of the means of reaching them. The main difference in this book is that it is the only systematic approach to constructing word-of-mouth campaigns, its unique description of word-of-mouth seminars, and expert management.

Again, if you are in marketing, you should read them all.

For additional references, visit www.mnav.com/resources.htm.

APPENDIX A

What Drives People to Web Sites

I interviewed Bernadette Tracy, President of NetSmart in June, 2000.* She produced what many people have called the definitive report on Internet usage. Here's what she had to say about what drives people to Web sites.**

In the 1990s, marketers were obsessed with banner ads: How to make them better, how to make them more noticeable, how to increase click-through rates, etc. At the end of the 1990s, banner ads lost their impact. Banner click-throughs dropped from 88 percent of people in 1995 (who have ever clicked on a banner in the past month), to 27 percent in 2000. Now the marketing world is moving toward content sponsorships, i.e., a portal advertising model to drive Web site traffic. In 2000, 46 percent visited a Web site in the last month as a result of sponsored content and hyperlinks on portals versus 27 percent from banner ads.

*Sadly, Bernadette Tracy died in November 2000, as this book was going to press. She was a major source of encouragement and a real "character" and inspiration. We'll all miss her.

**Interview based on The NetSmart VI Report, "Through the Looking Glass: Consumer Insights into the Cyber Future." Reprinted with permission.

Even search engines have lost their impact. Only 54 percent of respondents have visited a Web site in the last month as a result of a search or ad on a search engine. This is down from 76 percent in 1997.

The overlooked untapped opportunity is word of mouth. Fifty-five percent have visited a Web site in the last month based on word of mouth. This is up from 36 percent in 1996, when we first started tracking the impact of word of mouth. There are three reasons for this:

1. After a year, the people whom *Netsmart* calls the "Integrators" and "Trendsetters," have already bookmarked their favorite sites. The only opportunity for traditional online and offline advertising to make any kind of an impact are the "Newbies," who are still finding their way around.

2. On even the very best search engines, a very simple search can return hundreds or even thousands of irrelevant matches, discouraging people somewhat from using them.

3. The Internet has become so cluttered that the only way to break through the noise is word of mouth.

Word of mouth has reached a strategic inflection point. It is outpacing all the traditional online and offline advertising models.

In response to the question, "Why is word of mouth having such a dramatic impact?" she replied:

It's very simple. In the Old Economy word of mouth had a powerful but limited impact on a close circle of family and friends. When people had an extremely positive experience, they would tell two to three others. A negative experience generated about ten mentions. In the "Net

Economy," it's a whole new ballgame. E-mail is the coin of the realm. It's the most frequent online activity. Ninety-one percent of online users send and receive e-mail on a regular basis. And the big news from a word-of-mouth marketing viewpoint is that the typical online user has a 25- to 50-person e-mail list. And those in their e-mail list also have a 25- to 50-person e-mail list. So, we don't have to go further. You can visualize the domino effect of a positive or negative experience on your site.

I would point out that taking the more conservative number, $25 \times 25 \times 25 \times 25 \times 25 \times 25$ gives you 244,140,625, almost the entire population of the States. One more iteration and you reach 6,103,515,625, more than the population of the entire world! Not that everyone is reached, but the point is that only five or six iterations to a person's personal e-mail list reaches everyone who has e-mail with multiple "hits." I don't know about you, but when I realized this, I couldn't sleep that night. Think about its implications for you! Regarding the impact of word of mouth on specific product category Web sites, Tracy had this to say:

The percent of people who went to a Web site in the last month as a result of word of mouth ranges from 52 percent to 60 percent across all categories: high and low ticket items, packaged goods, pharmaceuticals, clothing, etc. This is across the board because of the clutter and unresponsive searches *and it does not vary by length of time online*. A point also worth noting is that the *Netsmart* "Newbies" (55 percent) and the *Netsmart* "Trendsetters" (54 percent) were equally likely to rely on the power of electronic word of mouth.

The key to triggering word of mouth on the powerful e-mail grapevine is to make sure your site offers something unique worth talking about.

APPENDIX B
The New Gatekeepers

Infomediaries want to help people regain their privacy online. They also want to play matchmaker between marketer and consumer.*

You can't blame consumers for feeling a bit paranoid online. With cookies racking their very click, it's no wonder they're worried about who's capturing their personal information—and what they're doing with it. A new study of 10,000 Web users by the Graphic, Visualization and Usability Center at the Georgia Institute of Technology found that 71 percent of respondents believe there should be laws to protect privacy on the Internet. A full 84 percent object to content providers reselling information about users to other companies.

Now there may be a way for people to turn their paranoia into profit. It centers around an "infomediary,"' an online broker that works on behalf of consumers. Much like storing important papers in a safe deposit box, individuals would entrust their personal profiles to an infomediary, and charge marketers for access to their data.

The infomediary would perform dual roles, gatekeeper and agent. "Slowly but surely, consumers are going to realize that their profile is valuable," says Mike Sheridan, vice president of strategic business at Novell, the Salt Lake City–based computer networking company. "For loaning out their identity, they're going to expect something in return." Experts say it's a win for consumers overwhelmed by raids on their privacy, and a win for marketers frustrated with dismal response rates. There's a potential downside for marketers as well. If the concept plays out, many companies could see their control over customer relationships slip into the hands of infomediaries.

Consider this scenario: A consumer informs her infomediary that she's shopping for a sports utility vehicle and that she'd like to learn about new models. The infomediary relays this message to SUV makers. Based on the consumer's expressed preferences, the infomediary discloses her basic demographic profile and instructs the companies to send ads to her by e-mail only (the woman hates to be interrupted by telemarketers during dinner). Working through the infomediary, the SUV-makers dispatch targeted e-mail promos to the consumer, hoping to woo her into their dealerships. The companies pay the infomediary for access to the consumer; the infomediary, in turn, rewards the consumer—maybe with cash or another incentive—for her time and attention.

Already a handful of start-ups are billing themselves as infomediaries. Last month, El Cerrito, California-based Lumeria debuted SuperProfile, an encrypted Web form that includes all of an individual's personal information— address, age, gender, income, credit card numbers, and so on. An opt-in service lets consumers pick and choose companies that wish to contact them about a particular product. Marketers pay an access fee to Lumeria, which passes on a substantial chunk—80 percent—to the consumer, says CEO Fred Davis.

PrivaSeek in Louisville, Colorado, touts a similar product. Users fill out a "persona" profile, and a software tool, dubbed the "valet," tracks the use of that data online. For example, the valet could automatically fill out Web forms with info culled from the persona and update the profile with transaction or clickstream data. PrivaSeek stores the persona in a secure Web facility (the company calls it the "vault"), with the consumer holding the key. "It's their own personal datamart," says PrivaSeek CEO Larry Lozon. "The consumer will be in charge of a brand called 'me.' " Like Lumeria, PrivaSeek will also play matchmaker between marketer and consumer, provided that the consumer wants to be courted. Neither company plans to advertise in the near future; for now, they hope viral marketing (a.k.a. word of mouth) will jumpstart their database.

But will consumers trust a start-up they've never heard of with all of their personal information? Doubts about security could plague new companies that promote even the most stringent policies on privacy. "In principle, it's possible to have honest brokers between a person and a corporation," says Amitai Etzioni, a social scientist at George Washington University and author of *Limits of Privacy*. "But you have to ask the question that Plato raised: Who's going to guard the guardians?"

Traditional companies, some experts contend, may be better suited to become infomediaries because they've spent years cultivating the trust of their customers. "The bricks-and-mortar guys may have a bigger card to play than they're currently given credit for," says Novell's Mike Sheridan. "They have a trusted brand."

Novell wants to help those trusted brands evolve into infomediaries. Citigroup and First USA, two leading financial-services companies, are currently testing Novell's digitalme product, which stores personal data, passwords and credit-card numbers for consumers. Digitalme users can update their profiles at any time and selectively unlock information for merchants, Web sites, and individuals. Testing digitalme makes sense, says Dan Schutzer, vice president of E-citi at Citigroup, because the company already plays an infomediary-like role. "If you're a Citibank customer today and you apply for a loan elsewhere," he says, "we're requested to provide information on your behalf to that third party."

Indeed, John Hagel, III and Marc Singer, principals at consulting firm McKinsey & Company, contend in their new book *Net Worth* that successful infomediaries will emerge from partnerships between nimble Internet-based businesses and traditional companies with large customer databases.

There's room for multiple infomediaries as well. Consumers might have a trusted agent for financial services, another for recreation, and still another for their healthcare needs. As the relationships strengthen over time, says Don Peppers, partner at consulting firm Peppers and Rogers Group in Stamford, Connecticut, there's more incentive for the consumer to stay loyal. "If he moved on, he'd have to re-teach the competitor what he's already taught you," Peppers says. Having a category focus will be important in the early stages of infomediaries, McKinsey's Hagel adds. "It will be difficult to approach customers from the start and say, 'Trust me. Now tell me everything about yourself,'" he says. Which categories are ripe for infomediaries? Hagel says cars, housing and healthcare.

Still, it's questionable whether a company in a particular industry could deliver unbiased information. Would American Airlines, if it were an infomediary, really promote a cheaper flight on Delta to its customers? "Companies are least credible in their own domains," says McKinsey's Singer.

In a world of infomediaries, what might be the consequences for business? More effective marketing is likely, since companies will be able to target consumers who've expressed interest in their product. Hagel and Singer suggest infomediaries will capture customer relationships— and that other companies will be forced to think about what data is most valuable about their consumers. Predicts Hagel, "The focus won't be on what data you own, but on how you use the data."

How to Conduct Employee Research

Although this section deals primarily with sales representative research, most of it equally applies to other kinds of employees as well. Why is this in a word-of-mouth book? Because your internal word of mouth is among the most important word-of-mouth messages that you can generate. If your employees are not enthusiastic, why should your customers be?

Why conduct employee research? After all, there is a regular reporting chain in most companies. Managers talk to their salespeople on a regular basis.

Paradoxically, while there are many formal mechanisms for *monitoring* employee performance, employees' *inputs* are also sadly neglected in most organizations. It is very difficult for management to spend enough time in the field, and very costly to bring salespeople, for instance, in from the field. Often, when information goes up the formal ladder, it gets filtered and distorted. That's why generals inspect the troops, but rarely as much as they would like to.

But sales and product managers spend time in the field with sales reps all the time.

When a sales manager does go into the field with a rep, the focus is usually on the rep's performance, or on the sales process itself, with little time for broader product issues. Almost totally neglected are advertising themes, sales materials, competitive issues, product positioning, what the salesperson has picked up about the word-of-mouth grapevine, or even widespread morale issues. The reps are on their best behavior. If there are problems caused by sales management itself, or by product management, it is unlikely that a sales manager or product manager will be able to spot them or correct them. For the same reason that you don't send salespeople out to do marketing research on your customers, you shouldn't send management out to do research on your salespeople.

Yet sales reps are a gold mine of information and creativity. It is crucial that you research them. They are part of marketing just as much as your product mix, your advertising, your packaging, your pricing, and your distribution. In fact, salespeople—and their associated materials, sales aids, handouts, and sales strategies—are usually the most important force in the marketplace, next to word of mouth. Salespeople are on the front line interacting with your customers and prospects all the time. *They spread word of mouth among themselves and hear it from customers.* They often know more about what is going on in the marketplace than anybody. However, they don't always know that they know it, and they are not always eager to communicate it.

How should this research be done?

The same considerations govern salesperson research as any other kind of marketing research. You do surveys (*quantitative* research) when you know what to ask and when you need to know something that has to be counted. You do *qualitative* research when the issues are more open-ended. *Most salesperson research of the type I have been describing should be qualitative.*

Should it be done individually, or in groups? Here, *the focus group is definitely the method of choice.* Individually, salespeople are often reluctant to reveal their secrets. In groups, they try to outdo each other. The very competitiveness that can shut down some groups (e.g., local physicians or local drugstore owners) makes salespeople open up. They want to show that they have a better way, they see that others have the same difficulties and are suddenly willing to talk about them, and they build on each others' ideas.

But these groups *should not contain salespeople from the same district* (unless you are zeroing in on the peculiarities of that district). If the salespeople are from the same district, they will be participating with the same people they are in meetings with all the time, they have certain roles to maintain, they are competitors, they all have the same boss, and they may be concerned that what they say will do them damage. The atmosphere of psychological safety that is a necessary condition to any focus group is usually destroyed. There are ways to get around this problem, but, fortunately it is not necessary.

The best way to conduct groups of salespeople from a widespread geographical area is by conducting telephone focus groups. I invite you to access my paper, "Questions and Answers about Telephone Focus Groups—and Answers from the Man Who Invented Them," on our Web site (www.mnav.com). Through PhoneFocus™ groups, salespeople can be brought together from a wide geographical area, in the early morning or in the evening, without losing travel time, or even without losing time from selling! The fact that they can't see each other creates additional psychological safety, further opening them up. The feeling of anonymity and informality is enhanced by the use of first names. Imagine doing groups of salespeople during a critical period—a product launch, a product recall, a competitive threat, adverse publicity—without losing a minute of sales time!

In most cases, *it is crucial to have an outsider do the sessions*, with a market research person (but no one else!) from the company listening in. An outsider not only brings objectivity, but further enhances psychological safety. Salespeople do not want to challenge management. They want to tell an outsider their difficulties, ideas, and suggestions, and have him or her transmit these to management in stronger language than they themselves could use. I continually hear remarks like, "I wouldn't dare tell management this, but put in your report that...." A third party can distance himself from management and get them to tell him about all sorts of things that they will not tell a company person. The outsider can bring the experience that comes from talking with dozens of different sales forces and can often spot morale issues, or other problems that an insider might miss. For instance, in role-playing sales interactions in many different situations, I often discover that the message that the salespeople and management think they are communicating is not the message being received by the prospect.

I'm continually amazed at how salespeople will openly discuss morale issues that I know they would not otherwise discuss. Also, an outsider can get them to see things from the perspective of management that they would interpret as excuse making from a company source, and get them to engage in constructive problem solving rather than argument.

Of course, a researcher has to be very experienced in talking with many different types of salespeople, and should have had sales experience himself. By having spent time in the field going around with salespeople and calling on customers, one has gained an appreciation for the realities of the sales situation. Under the proper conditions, an independent researcher will have salespeople falling all over themselves to make sure that management gets a clear picture of what is going on.

Tom Peters on Word of Mouth

What Tom Peters said about word-of-mouth marketing in his book *Thriving on Chaos*, published in 1987, was extremely prophetic. His comments, and those of Regis McKenna and Everett Rogers, were made *before the general and widespread acceptance of the Internet*. Therefore, their passionate advocacy of the importance of word-of-mouth marketing are all the more brilliant, while at the same time they are understandable underestimations of the present-day importance of word of mouth. I believe that this is an extremely important historical document.*

" . . . Since the exploding array of new products and services is causing more and more confusion in the marketplace, and in the minds of early buyers of industrial or consumer goods, we should:

■ Organize new-product/service marketing efforts around explicit, systematic, extensive word-of-mouth campaigns.

"Purchasers buy the new based primarily upon the perceptions of respected peers who have already purchased or tried the product. The twist this prescription adds is the idea that word-of-

*From *Thriving on Chaos* by Tom Peters. Copyright © 1987 by Excel, a California Limited Partnership. Reprinted by permission of Alfred A. Knopf, a division of Random House, Inc.

mouth campaigns for the new and untried can be as systematically pursued as can the use of traditional marketing tools, such as advertising. Such programs are increasingly important, as the number of competitors and their offerings increase exponentially, and their products' life cycles decrease dramatically. Influencing the early sorting-out process must be managed with great skill.

"Use systematic word-of-mouth campaigns as the keystone for launching all new products and services. The campaign should include specific and detailed strategies to land a half-dozen progressive (probably not big) customers prior to full-bore roll-out [emphasis his].

Make Word-of-Mouth Marketing Systematic

"Buying a new personal computer? Trying to figure your way through the jungle of new personal financial services? Where are you likely to go for counsel? Certainly you don't sit in front of the TV waiting for an ad to appear. And you're not likely to 'let your fingers to the walking.' You probably ask a respected friend, neighbor, or colleague who's been down the same route recently.

" . . . As a seller, you need not passively sit by.

"However, marketers tend to overrely on mass media advertising and underrely on the careful development of reputational campaigns, according to Regis McKenna. He goes on:

> Word of mouth is so obvious a communications medium that most people do not take time to analyze or understand its structure. To many people, it is like the weather. Sure, it is important. But you can't do much about it. You never see a 'word-of-mouth communications' section in marketing plans.... [Author note: Some of the largest corporations in the world, acknowledged leaders in marketing, are just beginning to require all marketing plans to set forth a word-of-mouth plan.]
>
> Of course, much of the word-of-mouth communication about a company and its products is beyond the com-

pany's control. But a company can take steps to put word of mouth to its advantage. It can even organize a 'word-of-mouth campaign.' ...The company must decide who should receive this message—and who from within the company should deliver it. By the nature of word-of-mouth communications, it is not possible to spread the message too widely. Luckily, there is no need to. Word of mouth is governed by the 90-10 rule: '90 percent of the world is influenced by the other 10 percent.' . . . A word-of-mouth campaign should be based on targeted communication. Word of mouth is not an efficient means for distributing information widely. . . .

The targets for a word-of-mouth campaign fall into several categories:

■ *The financial community.* Who backs a company is often more important than how much money is behind it.... A company's initial backers can use word of mouth to spread the company's message.

■ *Industry-watchers.* Rapid-growth industries are filled with consultants, interpreters, futurists and soothsayers who sort out and publish information through word of mouth....

■ *Customers.* Companies can use word-of-mouth to reach customers at trade shows, technical conferences, training programs, and customer organizations. [New-product test] sites and early customers become especially important.

■ *The press.* More than 90 percent of the major news stories in the business and technical press come from direct conversations. All journalists have networks of sources they use for background, opinions, and verification. It is valuable to become part of this word-of-mouth network.

■ *The selling chain.* The selling network includes sales representatives, distributors, and retailers.... Word of mouth is needed to generate enthusiasm and commitment toward the product.

■ *The community.* Every person who is interviewed, or delivers a package, or visits a company walks away with an impression. If company employees communicate properly, every person who comes in contact with the company becomes a salesperson for the company, a carrier of goodwill about the company.

"Ev Rogers of the University of Southern California is the leading expert on 'diffusion of innovation.' [He is now at the University of New Mexico. His book, *Diffusion of Innovations*, is must reading for anyone interested in word of mouth.] He has examined how new ideas and new products spread. His dozens of studies have analyzed new commercial products, the adoption of birth control techniques, and agricultural technology to determine the reasons behind the typical 30-year and 40-year delays in the widespread dissemination of innovations—delays which mark even products and services that demonstrate crystal-clear, decisive advantages from the start.

"Rogers, like McKenna, emphasizes the overriding power of networks: 'most individuals do not evaluate innovation on the basis of scientific study of its consequences. Most depend mainly upon a subjective evaluation of innovation that is conveyed to them from other individuals like themselves who have previously adopted the innovation. This dependence on the communicated experience of near-peers suggests that the heart of the diffusion process is the imitation by potential adopters of their network partners who have adopted previously.' Study after study that Rogers reviews reveals that: (1) an innovation takes off only after 'interpersonal networks have become activated in spreading subjective evaluations,' and (2) 'success is related to the extent that the change agent or marketer worked through opinion leaders.'

"I write, I must admit, with this zeal of a true believer. My first book, *In Search of Excellence,* was launched by an unsystematic (but in retrospect, thorough) word-of-mouth campaign. A 125-page presentation of what became the book's principal findings was first bound in 1980, fully two years before the book was published, and circulated surreptitiously among business executives. My co-author, Bob Waterman, and I eventually printed 15,000 (plus at least an equal number of photocopied knockoffs) presentation copies to meet the underground demand, much to the misguided consternation of our publisher, who was certain we were giving away most of our future sales. We also assiduously courted opinion leaders in the media over a period of several years. Thus within days of the book's launching, supportive reviews appeared, and the network of 15,000 (plus at least an equal number of photocopied knockoffs) hurried to buy the real thing, often in bulk for their subordinates. We could not have more effectively marketed the book if we systematized and planned for the process meticulously."

Getting Word of Mouth Organized

"The important point, to which McKenna speaks so passionately, is that the process can be systematized. For instance:

- Careful charting of official and unofficial opinion leaders can be conducted.

- Disproportionate selling time can and should be aimed at highly reputable, would-be early adopters.

- Sales incentives should encourage working with early adopters.

- Events that pair happy new customers with a wider audience can be staged on both a one-shot and an ongoing basis.

- User newsletters can be established, then circulated to targeted nonusers.

- Testimonials can be systematically gathered and circulated.

- All of these programs and others can be put together in a detailed, written, step-by-step "word-of-mouth" campaign plan.

The Search for Small, Progressive Buyers

"The most critical word-of-mouth activity is, of course, targeting early adopters. *Above all, look for the innovative adopters, not necessarily the big ones* [emphasis his]. Sure, you'd like to launch your new workstation by signing up GM. Yes, you'd like the chairman of the town's biggest firm to be the first to buy your new personal financial planning service. But such giants, though certainly helpful to word-of-mouth diffusion, are usually laggards when it comes to adopting new products and services. Therefore, you would be wise to look to smaller firms or individuals with a reputation for progressiveness; they're much more likely to become early adopters. Pouring almost all of your energy into getting a couple of these leaders on board is usually a worthwhile strategy.

First Steps

"Take one new product and ask these questions: (1) Am I devoting 75 percent of my marketing effort—dollars and energy—to activating a word-of-mouth network? (2) Are all of my salespersons devoting a specific—and sizable—share of time (and money) to user network development and expansion? Are they compensated for doing so? (3) Is *every* employee a conscientious network developer among his or her colleagues? Based upon the answers, develop a 60-day word-of-mouth blitz (targeted very precisely on a few key progressive customers) to relaunch or enhance product/service acceptance."

Word of Mouth in Practice: Promoting Paddi Lund's Book

When you buy Paddi Lund's book, *Building the Happiness Centred Business*, you get an option to receive an e-mail that gives the pertinent information about Paddi Lund and where to get the book (it isn't generally available). *It invites you to fill in your description at the top. Actually, you get two e-mails, one explaining the second. Here is the first message:

> Dear George,
>
> Thanks for asking about an e-mail referral card for Paddi's book, *Building the Happiness Centred Business*. Paddi's book has a wonderful message that really should, as one reader said, "be trumpeted to the world."
>
> And because it's not in bookstores, this is a great way to share Paddi's story. I'm sending you two e-mail messages including this one. The other is the e-referral card for you to forward to your friends.

*Reprinted with permission.

All you have to do is open that second message with the subject line: "A great book by a crazy Australian dentist...." In your e-mail window, press the "Forward" button or look for the "Forward" command. Then, add the e-mail address of your friends or business acquaintances who you feel would really benefit from Paddi's story.

Of course, it's more personal if you write to one person at a time, but you can put in multiple addresses if you want. Regardless, please take a moment to explain in as much detail as you can how you came to hear of Paddi's book, that it's not readily available, and why you liked it so much. Then send it off.

Now it's important to us that you feel good about recommending Paddi's book. If your friends come to us, we'll repay your faith by treating your friends well. We'll do all we can to make your friends very happy and grateful to you for the experience.

So, happy writing. We hope your friends enjoy reading about Paddi's insights and philosophies of business just as much as you have.

Kind regards,

Loretta Cohen
Solutions Press
149 Old Cleveland Road
Capalaba, Queensland
Australia 4157
www.solutionspress.com.au
Telephone (+61-7) 3823 3230
Facsimile (+61-7) 3390 3610

Here's what the second message looks like:

Please write your message to friends here. In the best way you know how, tell the story of Paddi and his book, how you heard of it and why you liked it so much. Then forward this message to those whom you really feel will enjoy Paddi's unique approach of happiness through simple systems in business.

Building the Happiness Centred Business

By Dr Paddi Lund

(RRP AUS$29.95, US$19.95, UK£15)

How you can find happiness in your business and reap all the rewards that it brings (including increased profits), by following in the footsteps of a crazy dentist.

Business, Happiness and Money Never Mixed...Until Now!

Building the Happiness-Centred Business is a little hard to find. You will only see it in a few specialty bookshops around the world. You can however purchase the book direct from the publisher for A$29.95 (UK £15, US$19.95) plus packaging of A$5 (A$10 overseas).

Please call on (+61-7) 3823 3230, or write with credit card details by facsimile on (+61-7) 3390 3610. You can also visit our Web site below, or write by e-mail to (info@solutionspress.com.au) with your phone number and address details. Please mention that you have received this e-card.

149 Old Cleveland Road, Capalaba, Qld 4157 Australia

Index